SHIP MODELS

[1] MODEL OF THE CLIPPER SHIP "SEA WITCH"
Built by Charles G. Davis

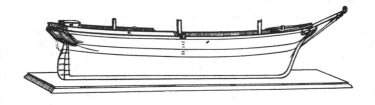

SHIP MODELS
HOW TO BUILD THEM

By CHARLES G. DAVIS
Naval Architect

ILLUSTRATED BY THE AUTHOR

Originally published by the Marine Research Society,
Salem, Massachusetts;
reprinted by special arrangement with the
Peabody Museum of Salem

DOVER PUBLICATIONS, INC.
New York

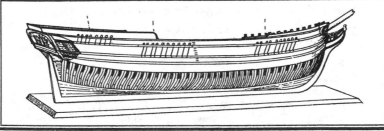

Published in Canada by General Publishing Company, Ltd., 30 Lesmill Road, Don Mills, Toronto, Ontario.
Published in the United Kingdom by Constable and Company, Ltd., 10 Orange Street, London WC2H 7EG.

This Dover edition, first published in 1986, is an unabridged republication of the work originally published as Publication Number Eleven of the Marine Research Society, Salem, Massachusetts, in 1925. The plates on pages xv–xxx, originally unbacked, are back-to-back in this edition. The present edition is published by special arrangement with the Peabody Museum, East India Square, Salem MA 01970.

Manufactured in the United States of America
Dover Publications, Inc., 31 East 2nd Street, Mineola, N.Y. 11501

Library of Congress Cataloging-in-Publication Data

Davis, Charles G. (Charles Gerard), 1870–1959.
  Ship models.

  Reprint. Originally published: Salem, Mass. : Marine Research Society, 1925. (Publication ; 11)
  Includes index.
  1. Ship models. 2. Sea Witch (Clipper-ship) I. Title.
VM298.D3 1986   623.8'201   86-6300
ISBN 0-486-25170-5

PREFACE

FOR many years there has been an increasing demand for a book on building models of sailing ships. The model yacht and the sailing boat have their manuals but necessary information relating to the various types of square-rigged vessels lies buried, here and there, in the pages of many volumes or remains unrecorded. The practical disappearance of the square-rigged ship and with it the passing of the old-time sailor who might supply the required information, also makes it exceedingly difficult for the builder of ship models to obtain first-hand information on those details so essential in constructing a model built to scale and correctly fitted and rigged. It was with great satisfaction, therefore, that the Marine Research Society at last found a man who was not only competent to write a book on model building and make the drawings necessary to illustrate the same, but willing to undertake the task.

Mr. Davis has had an unusual training. A naval architect by profession he has built many types of vessels and during the World War he superintended the construction of a score or more of large ships. The many line engravings in the following pages attest to his ability as a draftsman and also to his knowledge of every step in the actual construction of a sailing ship. And this familiarity with the old-time ship is based not only upon a technical training but also upon a practical experience gained while a seaman on board merchant vessels engaged in foreign trade.

This volume supplies complete instructions as to proper equipment and the various progressive steps to be taken in the laying out and construction of the hull and fittings. The clipper ship "Sea Witch" has been selected as a typical vessel to build in model form and in a pocket at the end of the volume will be found scale plans supplying exact lines for the hull and also a sail plan.

While this volume gives the dimensions for the masts and yards it does not cover the subject of rigging. That properly belongs to another volume and full information may be obtained in Biddlecombe's *Art of Rigging,* published by this Society in 1925.

Many friends have encouraged the preparation and publication of this volume and thanks are particularly due to Mr. William E. Northey, Mr. Malcolm B. Stone, Dr. Carl M. Vogel, Mr. Irving R. Wiles, and to the officers of the Peabody Museum, Salem.

CONTENTS

A SHIP OF 1850

INTRODUCTION

TO a man interested in ships, model building is a great pleasure. It calls for the exercise of a great deal of patience and considerable skill to produce a miniature ship so accurately as to look exactly like the original vessel, and a person just starting in at model making must not expect in his first attempt to produce a masterpiece.

It is far better to build something simple at first, just as a child enters the primary grade at school and works up; because there is a lot to learn in the building of a model ship that one cannot realize until he actually comes to do the work.

If the model is to be merely a recreation in its making, with little or no regard for accuracy, it is quite a simple matter to make something that looks like a ship; but the lure, the enchantment in building these tiny ships is in the ever-increasing desire to produce one more accurate, more "ship-shape and Bristol fashion," as sailors say, than the one previously made. Even after you can make a model of a ship and get correctly the proportions and shapes of spars and hull there is ever a goal ahead to strive for, for then you come into the advanced grade where no detail is too small to incorporate into your model — where the painting alone is almost an art.

Some say black paint is black paint and if a ship is painted that color there is nothing to it but black, and so they paint their models to look like a newly polished pair of shoes, even putting on shiny enamels. This spoils a ship model. You can imagine how a painting of a landscape would look if an artist were to follow the same rule.

It is the trick of mixing colors and the application of them as well that makes one model look like a toy and the other like a real ship. The model should show that worn appearance that ships' planking always has with, maybe, just a touch here and there as if rust had run down her sides; and when you paint the sides do so with a small brush and short strokes with once in a while a touch of red, or some other color, ever so little, mixed into the black to give it what artists term "vibration." We all know that grass and trees are green; but if you look off into the distance, over a hilly country, you will notice that the very atmosphere you look through makes them look bluer and lighter blue the farther off they are, until at the most distant point they are almost grey.

So get out of the primary grade and paint your ship as if it were a real, living picture instead of a picture on canvas and your models will assume a far more natural appearance than if primary, flat colors alone were used.

Stain the blocks to get away from that suggestion of brand-new wood. Stain your running rigging for the same reason and tone everything about the ship so as to look as it does in real life. Blacken the chains. Nothing is so raw looking as a shiny piece of brass chain for bob-stays and other head rigging. I don't mean to try and make her a fake antique — that is quite another practice. But do try to make her look as real ships look.

It is like working out a puzzle with the added charm that when you have done you have produced something that you can admire for years after and something that is an ornament as well, a most suggestive attraction in any room.

A ship model in a room suggests immediately a connection with the sea and all the mysteries that go with a seafaring life. Some ancestor, perhaps, followed the sea and the attic may reveal an old sea chest with curios from far-off lands. It may suggest a life in the days of the famous clipper ships, those proud mistresses of the seas that logged fourteen, fifteen or sixteen knots an hour through the water and hung onto their royal-studding sails when the ordinary ship had her topgallant sails furled to keep from driving bows under water; or it may be a pirate schooner, a slaver, or a ship away back in the sixteenth century, such as the old caravals with their quaint high bows and sterns and odd lateen yards with flags flying from every masthead.

A model doesn't have to be a perfect specimen of naval architecture to be attractive. Many an old sailor has toiled for months, in his idle moments at sea, to build a model of the ship he was on. He has not always the necessary tools and materials at hand to make all the parts he wishes to reproduce. Sometimes, as on whalers, ivory has been patiently worked down from the bone to represent the blocks and deadeyes for the model and while the hull may not be perfect, and the spars may be too heavy, yet the fact remains that what is shown on such a model represents an actual vessel of that date and that is where many facts in regard to the deck arrangements, the location and style of windlass that was used, and how the boats were carried, together with many old styles of rigging detail, are shown as they were at that particular date.

There is a large variety to pick from in choosing the type of ship one wishes to make a model of; just as there are all kinds of wagons from a hansom phaeton to a two-wheel cart. Ships have similar classifications. There are the fighting ships, men-of-war as they are called, and merchant ships. These are of different shapes and sizes, according to their era, and are rigged with a different number of masts and yards.

So the first step in building a model is to select a design, if such can be had, or a picture of the proposed ship.

HERMAPHRODITE BRIG

MODELS OF VESSELS

SIXTEEN PLATES ILLUSTRATING MODELS
OF DIFFERENT PERIODS

A CLIPPER SHIP

[2] THE "SANTA MARIA" — SHOWING CONSTRUCTION — 1492
Model in the Science Museum, South Kensington, London

[3] ELIZABETH GALLEON, 1580-1600
Model in the Science Museum, South Kensington, London

[4] THE "MARY," ADMIRALTY YACHT, 1673

Model in pearwood, owned by Col. H. H. Rogers, now in the Metropolitan
Museum of Art, New York

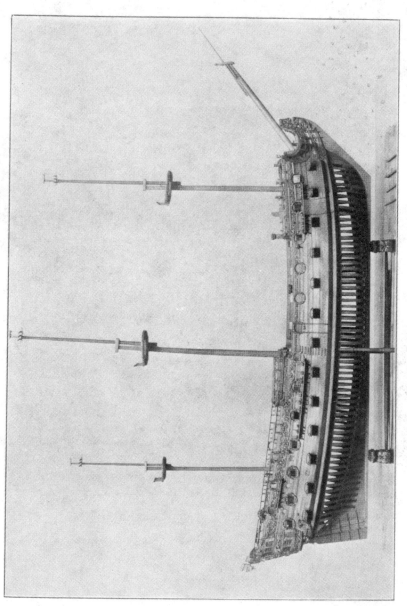

[5] H. M. S. "CHESTER," FOURTH-RATE MAN-OF-WAR, 1691

Model in the Science Museum, South Kensington, London

[6] 64-GUN SHIP BUILT FOR THE ENGLISH NAVY ABOUT 1750
Model in Science Museum, South Kensington, London

[7] H. M. S. "AMERICA," 44 GUNS, BUILT AT PORTSMOUTH, N. H., IN 1749
Model in the Portsmouth Athenæum, Portsmouth, N. H.

[8] ENGLISH SHIP-RIGGED SLOOP-OF-WAR, 1780
Model in Science Museum, South Kensington, London

[9] 64-GUN SHIP BUILT FOR THE ENGLISH NAVY, 1780-1790
Model in Science Museum, South Kensington, London

[10] MODEL OF AN AMERICAN FISHING SCHOONER, PERIOD OF 1820

Model in Marine Room, Peabody Museum, Salem

[11] CLIPPER SHIP "ANN McKIM," 493 TONS, BUILT AT BALTIMORE, MD., IN 1832

The first clipper ship built on the lines of the famous Baltimore clipper brigs and schooners. Model built by a Boston collector .

[12] AMERICAN SHIP OF 1830-1840. MODEL MADE ABOUT 1850 AND NOW IN THE
PEABODY MUSEUM, SALEM

[13] CLIPPER SHIP "RED JACKET," 2006 TONS, BUILT AT ROCKLAND, ME., IN 1854

Model built by a Boston collector.

[14] CLIPPER SHIP "STONEHOUSE," 1,153 TONS, BUILT AT PALLION, SCOTLAND, IN 1866
Model in the Science Museum, South Kensington, London .

[15] ENGLISH SHIP "CYGNET," ON LAUNCHING WAYS. BUILT IN 1870

Model in Science Museum, South Kensington, London

[16] AMERICAN COASTING SCHOONER "M. C. AMES"
Model in the collection of Clarkson A. Collins, Jr.

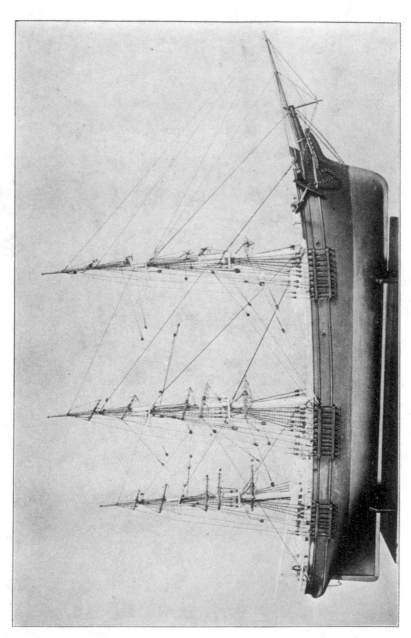

[17] SHIP "PANAY" OF SALEM, 1,190 TONS, BUILT AT BOSTON IN 1877

Model built by William E. Northey; now in Peabody Museum, Salem

SHIP MODELS

A NEW ENGLAND BARK

SHIP MODELS: HOW TO BUILD THEM

CHAPTER I

Types of Ships

TO the inexperienced all ships look alike and in later years steamships have been duplicated over and over again, many times, from the same set of plans, so that they are alike except for name. But in the days of sailing craft this duplication was not carried on so extensively and even if the hulls of several vessels were alike there were distinguishing features about the spars or rigging or deck houses that enabled those who knew to pick out each individual ship.

Just as one who knows automobiles can tell at a glance the make of a car, so shipping men could tell Bath-built ships from New York ships and Baltimore ships from New York ships, etc.; and just as styles in everything else changed so did ships and by a certain feature in the ship's hull the approximate year in which she was built can be told, just as in motor cars.

So, in making up a model, if you wish to build a ship of the year 1800 you should learn the features that were characteristic of the vessels of that date and not incorporate in her details that were not invented or used on ships until 1850.

It is a subject far beyond the scope of this book to describe all the various types, sizes and rigs of ships that have been built from ancient times up to the present, in order to give a list to choose from. There are many books published that give this information and from these one can pick the particular ship of which he wishes to build a model.

One thing to bear in mind is the fact that ships have gradually, year by year, increased in size and when we speak of a ship in the twentieth century, when sailing ships are built from two to three hundred feet long, it is hard to realize that in the early part of the seventeenth century there were ships as small as seventy-five feet in length; and as late as 1811 the "Mount Vernon," built in Massachusetts for New York owners, was a ship only 99 feet, 6 inches long, 28 feet wide, and of 352 tons burden. It is no wonder the skysails carried by the large clipper ships of later years were then unknown, for her spars aloft would be too light, if in proportion to the rest of the ship, for a man to trust his life going out on them.

The large war ships in the English, French and Dutch navies in the 18th century were ships of only about one hundred and fifty feet in length; so be careful in building old-time models that you do not make them look like ships of double their size.

Caravals and clipper ships, two extreme types, seem to be the most popular just now among model makers and there are more "Santa Marias," "Half Moons" and "Flying Clouds" being built today than any other type of ship.

The caravals do make a very pretty ornament with their high bows and sterns decorated in colors and with the picturesque combination of square sails and lateen sails, with colored flags and streamers from mastheads and peak and, moreover, their rigging is not so complex as a clipper's.

But the greatest eyesore of all to a shipbuilder is the total disregard for symmetry shown by some model

builders. They know very well that in a house no house builder would think of slanting his windows as shown in the accompanying diagram (Fig. 18), yet when they build a caraval they

Fig. 18

commit just as grievous an error when
on a ship where everything is slanting
and tapering and the vertical members
all show a radial, fan-like effect, they
put in square, house-like windows

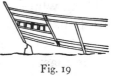

Fig. 19

Fig. 20

(Fig. 19). One is as bad as the other for the
same reason that the house windows should be
vertical to match the square, vertical effect of
the house (Fig. 20). The windows in the caraval should radiate on a slant to match
the adjoining members of the ship (Fig.
21). There is no trade in the world
where the mechanics employed strive

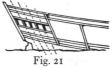

Fig. 21

to harmonize the various members used in construction,
as do shipbuilders, even to the gradual taper given every
plank and rail in the ship's side so that the ends of the
ship will not appear clumsy but look light and graceful.

Clipper ships were the acme of perfection in shipbuilding, speed and strength being apparent from their appearance. Their hulls, stripped of all the antique carv-
ings and elaborate ornamental work that made an old-
time ship's stern look like a lover's valentine, and with
all the carved trailboards, head rails, knees and high
carved figurehead of the stem gone, she looked like an
athlete stripped for action. The stern carried up sharp
and high ended in a very narrow or shallow stem, sometimes round instead of the old square style with nothing
but her name and hailing port in gilded letters thereon,
while the bow was equally bare. Sometimes a carved
dragon or figure symbolic of her name adorned the upper
end of her narrow cutwater that flared up close under
the bowsprit. They loaded deep in the water and had
a lofty set of spars, carrying three skysail yards and
studding sail booms to the royals.

Their white holystoned decks were less encumbered with houses than their predecessors the packet ships, giving a cleaner appearance on deck fore and aft.

The masts were spaced wide apart with the foremast well aft for the clippers had long, sharp bows, the waterline showing quite a hollow and the flam or flare of the bows up to the catheads on the topgallant forecastle being excessive.

The packet ships were about the most picturesque of all. They carried big rigs including skysails and studding sails and while the models were fined up a little below water in an effort to get speed, for these ships were the passenger and mail carriers before steamships supplanted them, they still retained in their topsides all the picturesque features that make a model look so shippy and interesting. Their sterns were highly ornamented and their bows carried carved figureheads, trail boards and head rails, while along their sides was painted that broad, white band with painted gun ports that at a distance made them look like a man-of-war.

On deck the early packets were small, flush-decked ships which was the common style in merchantmen until about 1812 when poop decks and forecastle heads were added. The crew's quarters were still below, down in the fore-peak, but the long boat, stowed in chocks between the main-hatch and the foremast, housed over and used to stow the pigs, chickens and geese, with the cowhouse lashed on top of the main-hatch, make a very interesting model and one that marks an epoch in our national marine, a record well worth preserving. The poop deck extended just forward of the mainmast, the main cabin below having its thwart-ship bulkhead set back forming a shelter deck below, with ladders on each side coming up through hatchways, giving access to the poop forward; while aft there was a wheel-house from which a gangway led down into the after cabin.

After the clippers there came, about 1860, a type of so-called semi-clippers where the hulls were filled out to give greater cargo capacity and labor-saving devices such as winches, donkey engines and double topsails came into vogue as freight rates declined and economy cut down the number of foremast hands the ships could afford to carry. They were large ships with poop decks, deck-house and forecastle heads; the crews being housed in a long, narrow house abaft the foremast in which also were the carpenter shop, galley, and if they carried power, the donkey boiler and hoisting engine with winch heads extending out on either side for hoisting topsails, etc. The two long boats were stowed bottom up on skids on top of the house.

Another picturesque type of model is that of a whale ship with all its quaint, clumsy-looking wooden davits, whale-boats, "cutting in" stage, with boat platform and gear house built across the stern forming a box on each quarter of the ship. The hulls of these ships might be almost any type of ship as old merchantmen, packet ships, etc., when worn out in their particular trade generally degenerated into "blubber-hunters," as sailors scornfully termed whalers.

CHAPTER II

Kinds of Models

SHIP models are constructed in a variety of ways according to the purpose for which they are to be used.

Some models only represent the ship above water and the boards upon which they are mounted are painted to imitate water or a mirror or ripple glass, as it is called, is used to simulate water. To make such a model does not require a very thick piece of wood, particularly if only the ship's hull to the deck is shaped from it and then the bulwarks built up afterwards.

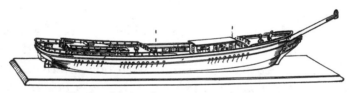

Fig. 22. Model of a hull above the water-line

Such models appeal to the old deep-water sailors. That is all they generally saw of ships and models so made reminded them more nearly of their former abiding places than did the full model. The technicalities associated with the shape of the ship's hull below the waterline, the angle of deadrise to the midship frame, how lean or how full-bodied she was below water, how sharp or how blunt in the ends, were to them uninteresting; but the ship above water, with every detail of deck houses, spars and rigging, was their favorite way of making a model. As a household ornament people usually prefer these models, particularly if they have those cleverly carved sails that make a ship look as if she were actually sailing "like a homeward bounder in the south-east tides."

Along in the 1880's, deep-water sailors used to whittle out sets of sails for model ships, made so that they could be nailed to a board from which they stood out at an angle of about forty-five degrees. The board was painted to represent sky and sea and sometimes further embellished with the cliffs of Dover, Cape Horn, or some well-known headland, island, or lighthouse. Half a ship's hull, above water, was then carved out and fitted below these sails on a sea made of putty or painted to represent water and placed on a narrow baseboard set at right angles to the backboard.

Other sides, making a shallow box like a shadow box on an oil painting, were then fitted and sometimes a glass front was put on to protect the model.

Another interesting kind of trick model was the ship-in-a-bottle, which causes much speculation as to how a full-rigged ship could be made inside a glass bottle. How was it put in? Was it rigged after it was put in? If so, how? Such are the questions provoked by these models. These models were usually all rigged before being inserted in the bottle. The masts were then laid down on deck in which position the whole model could be pushed into the bottle and by pulling up on the headstays the masts would be raised again into place. The headstays would then be glued fast, cut off and the cork inserted.

These models, like those made so microscopic in size that you need a glass to see the details, are not valuable as historic records of ships, but are merely curios. Some that I have seen were truly wonderful exhibitions of patience and a very few, besides being tiny, were accurate in their details, having deadeyes with lanyards properly rove — so tiny that a magnifying glass was needed to see them; but such work will ruin a man's eyesight. A model as small as ⅛ of an inch to the foot is small enough and about as small as can be made with accuracy. A larger scale is preferable.

White pine can be purchased as thick as four inches, but if difficulty is encountered in obtaining what is wanted, then take two boards, plane the adjoining surfaces smooth and glue them together. I have tried hot glues and cold glues, hoof glue and fish glue and what not, but now I use plain glue, generally Le Page's. The more important part in gluing wood together is to have the wood dry, slightly warm, rather than cold. Spread the glue evenly and then clamp it tightly together and

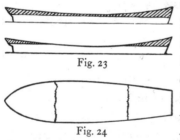

Fig. 23

Fig. 24

hold it so for a day at least before trying to use it. Try and have the top layer of wood so thick that the sweep or sheer of the deck, as it scoops down in the middle, will not cut through the upper layer of wood and leave thin edges (Fig. 23), as they are liable to come loose and curl up in time. There is a way of preventing this, which is by putting on a thin board over all to act as a deck (Fig. 24). When this is done these ends are of course held down and are completely hidden.

It is well-nigh impossible nowadays to obtain white pine in a block large enough to cut out a full model of a ship in one piece, unless she is to be made to a very small scale.

And it is not at all necessary that it should be so for you can take as many clear, soft, straight-grained pine boards as are needed to make up the size of the block your model requires and spread each with a layer of glue.

Then clamp all tightly together (Fig. 25) and you have what is called a bread and butter model. The principal point to observe in this sort of a model is to see that adjoining boards do not have the grain running at too great a variance from each other, as it will be found difficult to cut, if such is the case.

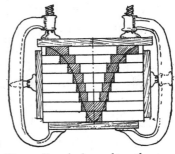

Fig. 25. Boards clamped together to make a "bread and butter" hull model.

Do not try to include the keel, stern and stern post. Model your hull only to the rabbet line — the seam on the ship where the planking joins the keel, stern, stem, etc., and later on add these members to the hull.

A full model of the ship, showing both sides, is preferable where one is more or less a student of ship development, as the underwater portion underwent many changes, from time to time, as ships increased in size. In 1770 a ship a hundred feet long was about the aver-

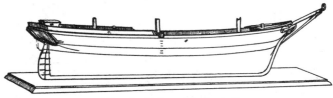

Fig. 26. Full model of a hull

age length as then built; but in 1850 ships were built nearer two hundred feet long and many were nearly three hundred. Some that were built to load cotton at New Orleans were built very flat in the bottom in order to draw as little water as possible in getting over the bar at the mouth of the Mississippi River. They were as square-sided as a box and built full in the ends in order to stow as many bales of cotton as could be jammed into them with huge screw jacks, for the cotton was so light for its bulk that the ship would be full and yet not sink very deep in the water. The packet ships that made regular trips back and forth across the Atlantic carrying passengers and mail with a little freight, if it could be had, but sailing on certain advertised dates throughout the year, doing what passenger steamers do in later years, were cut away to a much finer model below water and built to carry a press of sail.

The cargo carriers — old kettle-bottomed ships, as they were called—were big and wide near the bottom with the sides narrowing in at the deck, so as to cheat the tonnage measurement in vogue about 1830. Beam, one of the measurements used in computing the ship's tonnage for taxation, was measured at the deck and this was the cause of ships being built that were clumsy looking craft, even if they did earn more dollars for their owners.

When the California gold rush of 1849 came on and speed above everything else was demanded, the heretofore clumsy, full-bodied hulls were supplanted by a sharper-sectioned ship with very fine sharp ends that could reel off its fourteen to sixteen knots, but carrying less cargo, the profits being made up to the owners by the much higher rates paid for quick passages.

The advantage of the full-block model is that all these features of the ship can be expressed in the model.

The shipbuilder always cut out such a model, but for the sake of economy, as it answered all his needs, he only modeled one side of the ship, the other side being merely a duplicate reversed. Such models were called half models (Fig. 27), and years ago they were very numerous. Every shipping house, broker's office, and even shore-front saloons, had its walls decorated with these models mounted on highly polished boards of mahogany, black walnut or maple. Only a year ago I had the pleasure of viewing a collection of about thirty such builder's half models on the wall of what once was the office of the Mallory shipyard at Mystic, Conn. At Webb Academy, Fordham

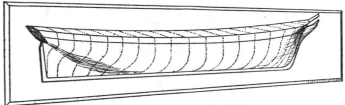

Fig. 27. Half model of a hull

Heights, New York, the ship models of William H. Webb are still preserved, and in the Smithsonian Institute at Washington there is a collection of such builder's models of all types of ships built from Maine to the Chesapeake that is historically invaluable. Other collections may be seen at the Peabody Museum, Salem, and at the Marine Museum in the Old State House, Boston.

Where the various boards, or lifts, as the shipbuilders term them, were joined together, the seam-traced lines that gave an indication of the ship's shape, corresponding to the various level or water-lines that are used in drawing up the lines of a ship—the plans from which it is built, and in the old days when such knowledge of ships' shapes was common talk along the waterfront and the terms, water-lines, buttocks and cross-sections, formed the topic of many a dinner hour discussion — these seams in the model were made more pronounced by mixing black with the glue, so that a distinct black line was made. Some builders sawed the blocks vertically in layers to show the shape of the buttock lines and one even went so far as to saw the model transversely at intervals to show the shape of the cross-sections or frames.

This practice led to the introduction of thin layers of veneer just the thickness of the saw cut. Another way of showing the lines of the ship more clearly was to make

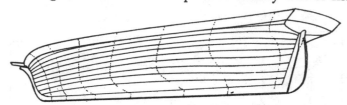

Fig. 28. Full hull model showing lifts

the lifts alternately of pine and mahogany or some other dark-colored wood, so that the shape of each water-line was clearly defined when the model was varnished.

One of the oldest "bread and butter" style of half models I have seen is in the New York Historical Society's building in New York. Painted upon the board on which this model is mounted is this inscription "Original Ship Model made by Orlando B. Merrill of Belleville, New-buryport, Mass^ts in 1796 and by the inventor now 90 years of age given to David Ogden of New York in Feb^ry 1853 who presented it to the New York Historical Society, 1853."

The lifts of this model are held accurately in place without glue by means of a key-shaped, wooden wedge fitting into a mortise cut vertically across the inner face of the lifts.

By removing a couple of screws which held this model to the board, I was able to pull out this wooden wedge which released the lifts so that I could lay them down separately on paper and trace their shapes by drawing a pencil around the curved edges of each, one at a time. With these shapes the plan of this ship can be reproduced.

That is why the shipbuilder so built it. Some merely screw each lift together adding one on top of another. But the advantage of this wooden, wedge-shaped key was that it made each lift fit perfectly in place. I have seen other models where this was accomplished by threading the lifts on two vertical, parallel dowels, sometimes of wood and sometimes of metal.

The screws holding each lift in place are an advantage in one way, for, as the model gets old, the lifts have a tendency to separate as the wood ages and dries and the screws keep them more snugly in place.

The lifts of a block model put together with glue are supposed to hold together indefinitely, but Nature will in time destroy anything and to help the glue to do its work it is a good practice to brad each lift together after you have the model shaped, then punch the nail in and fill the hole with putty or glue and sandpaper dust.

Only recently I was asked to look at a most beautifully made little model of an old three-decked battleship, made out of boxwood, that was about a hundred to a hundred and fifty years old and which had recently been imported from England where it had held its shape perfectly.

It was mounted on a mirror to represent water; set up on two pedestals and was under a glass case. This model that had lasted so well in the damp, wet climate of England had, on being exposed to the extreme dry heat we have in America, warped so that the ship was hump-backed. The lifts, of which the hull was made, were separating and had put such a pressure on the forward pedestal that the glass had cracked in all directions radiating from the pedestal. Boxwood, one of the hardest and most enduring of all woods, had been used in making this beautifully executed model in order to make it last forever and yet Nature, through the medium of moisture and heat, was ruining it. It is to prevent this that you see small vials or jars of salt placed inside glass cases where expensive models are kept.

In making solid block models precaution should be taken to see that dry, seasoned wood is used or you may have the same result. Your model may crack and split. Hollow the model out so it is only about half an inch thick and you will lessen this liability to warp and check by reducing the bulk of wood that expansion and contraction acts upon.

A very effective model is made by first making a block model, leaving the sides fairly thick, and then nailing thin, narrow planks on the outside so to all appearances when done it looks like a built-up model. To do this correctly one must study how ships are planked. They are not merely parallel strips, but like the tapered staves of a barrel are wider in the middle than at the ends; and five or six planks from the deck down and about three up from the keel they are made of thicker material. If the ship be an old-timer, such as a seventeenth century man-of-war, there are many more heavy strakes worked into the planking.

Another fake way of building up a model is to cut out several moulds to give the shape of the ship and using a little thicker wood to plank up the sides over these moulds. But to do it right is far more satisfactory if you are going to make a built-up model. Build her just as the ship was built, excepting, of course, that you can make the keel of one stick instead of several short ones. Each frame is formed and fastened in place along the keel and then some, but not all, of the side planks are put on (Fig. 29). The advantages of not planking it all up solid are, that it shows the pains one has gone to in the construction of the model, which otherwise would all be hidden; and what is more important it allows air to circulate through it freely, thereby preventing dry rot which has caused many a tightly closed model to crumble into dust prematurely.

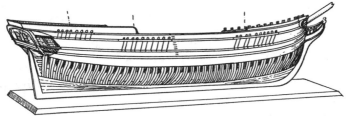

Fig. 29. Framed model partly planked

In England it was the custom for shipbuilders to prepare and present with their plans a small built-up replica of any newly proposed class of ships in order that the Lords of the Admiralty, who were perhaps none too well versed in the reading of ships' plans, might the better realize just what the new ships were to look like. It is these so-called Admiralty models, much sought after by collectors, that many try to imitate, but the experienced shipbuilders can soon detect the errors that stamp them as copies.

CHAPTER III

Preparing the Block

IF you are going to build your block model from a plan, you will need templates to guide you in shaping the hull, to make certain that you are making it the shape that the plan shows and also to have both sides alike.

The quickest way is to make a tracing from the plans of the ship drawn to a scale that gives you just the size you want to make it. With the modern method of photostat process this is a very simple matter. You can take a large plan and have it reduced to any size or a small one and have it enlarged to the size you want.

Either trace this plan on tracing linen, to prick through, or, with a sharp awl or needle prick right through the photostat onto a piece of cardboard and so obtain the shape of your ship's sections. A coat of white shellac will soon harden your card templates after they are cut out so that they will be stiffer and easier to work with. Some persons prefer templates made of sheet zinc or tin and work them to the exact shape with a file after first cutting them out with shears.

Make a template of each end of the ship from the side-elevation or sheer-plan, to the rabbet-line — the seam where the ends of the planking butt against the stem at the bow and the stern-post aft. This rabbet-line also runs from bow to stern along the top edge of the keel where the bottom planking joins the keel. If the figure-head is very prominent, make also a template of the outline of the cutwater clear from the forefoot at the keel to the billet-head or figurehead under the bowsprit. That profile cannot be made too carefully for like a person's face, it expresses the whole character of the design.

Then for the cross-section templates you will need one amidships or mid-length of the vessel; one close to each end; and one or two between, depending on whether the ship's lines are easy or have a quick curve to them. Better to have one template too many than not enough to check up on the shape of the hull as you cut it.

In using templates be careful that you apply them at the correct spot and at the same angle they represent in the plan. Square up the block of wood you are going to cut the model out of and draw a center line around all four faces (two faces top and bottom and two ends). Space off on this line the frame stations you have selected and made templates of and then square those marks around on all four sides of the block. Then, as you cut away on one side, you will have the marks on the other by which you can locate and redraw the section on which to try the template.

Don't carelessly cut away the marks and fail to replace them for that is the way models are made lop-sided. Keep checking up as you work to see that the model is true.

If there is a woodworking shop nearby much time and hard work can be eliminated by marking out (Fig. 30) the profile of your ship on one side and the greatest breadth plan on the top (be sure and allow for the swell of the sides which in ships is generally greater than the shape on the deck) and sawing these out

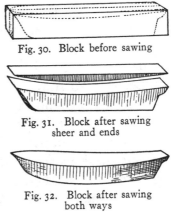

Fig. 30. Block before sawing

Fig. 31. Block after sawing
sheer and ends

Fig. 32. Block after sawing
both ways

with a band saw. As you saw out the sheer of the deck or rail you will cut off the part that has the half breadth marked upon it (Fig. 31), so lay it back and brad it fast temporarily until you saw out the shape of the sides (Fig. 32).

With a block model so cut out you are now ready to begin to cut it away until each template fits accurately in its proper location.

There is another method of building block models — not solid, one-piece ones, but the bread and butter models — that the novice will perhaps find easier after all the sawing out is done. That is, to lay out the shape of each water-line shown in the plan on boards just the thickness of the spacing between the water-lines and on each board to trace out the shape of the water-line it represents. Saw them all out and if you have a jig saw it's a good plan to saw out as much of the inside as will leave you at least half an inch of wood on each seam after the model is all shaped up.

This requires a clear head and some care in laying out the lifts so as not to make a mistake, for the bevels are so varied that you may cut out too much and not realize it until you have cut clear through in shaping the outside of the ship. To prevent this, lay out the shape of the water-line represented by the top of the board and also the water-line represented by the bottom surface of the board. It is neglecting to do the latter that causes the trouble. As an index use some certain mould, say the midship section, and lay each water-line out from that point, for if they are not placed accurately your ship will come out very unfair.

When these various lifts are all sawed out, save the pieces you cut off the outside and after gluing the edges of the lifts that make up the block to be cut, pack all the outside pieces back in place so that you have a square block again and you will find it an easy matter to hold each lift in its proper place and also easier to clamp all together until the glued portion dries (Fig. 25).

You may find the addition of the glue between the edges of the parts you want to stick together will increase their depth so that there is a noticeable difference between them and the unglued portion. If this is too pronounced, lay pieces of paper between the unglued layers, but don't insert so much as to prevent squeezing down hard on the glue, and above all see that the vertical center marks on each end are in a true line up and down. Don't allow a lift to slip over to one side a little and so throw the ship out of true. That is where packing the cut off pieces back in place will aid you. If they are all put together and squared up into a squared block before being cut and care is taken to lay them out evenly from each side, they will squeeze back into a true block again and give you a fair ship.

Put smooth-surfaced pieces of stout boards under the toes of the iron screw clamps unless you can get the flat joiner clamps which will of themselves straighten the lifts out true.

When this block has been allowed to stand and the glue has hardened for twenty-four hours you will have a block that looks like a pair of steps and each corner is an accurate guide to cut to. All you now have to do is to round off the projecting corners and the ship is modeled except at the extreme ends near the top of the deck and there you will have to be very careful and not cut away too much, for the shape of the counters aft and the extreme flare forward will require you to make one or two extra templates unless you can read a plan well enough to shape it by eye with a few measurements.

Supposing we were so situated that we had no plans, no data of any kind and yet with leisure and inclination to build a little model of a ship, how would we go about it? Many men have found themselves in this predicament and have gone blindly ahead and made a model, too many of which show it, and for all the work put in it is a pity that they were not better guided in their efforts.

We will now take the clipper ship "Sea Witch" and describe how she may be reproduced in a small model. She was one of the first clipper ships built and the most extreme of them all in point of fineness of model, having considerable rake to her masts, more than was customary in 1846, when she was launched. For three years she was "Mistress of the Seas." They only beat her by building vessels much larger in size. She made several voyages around the world, going out from New York to California and so on to China from which she brought home cargoes of tea. She was eventually wrecked March 26, 1856, on the eastern end of Cuba.

To make this model you will need a block of wood 23 inches long, 4¼ inches wide and 3⅛ inches thick. This is ⅛ inch less than the total depth of the ship as shown on the plans, but this will be made up by a ¼ inch thick board forming the deck, which is reduced to ⅛ inch at the edges to give the crown, or round, to the deck.

Lay out the shape shown in Fig. 33 and saw it out with a band-saw. If no such convenience is at hand, first lay out the side plan (Fig. 34), and cut the deck sheer first,

Fig. 33. Shape of the model

laying out the shape of the deck on this surface when you have the sheer shaped perfectly sweet and fair with no humps showing when viewed end on. You may not notice the humps

and hollows viewing it side-
ways, but when foreshortened
they become instantly apparent to the eye.

Fig. 34.   Side plan

I have shaped many a model by gripping it between
my knees and cutting the sheer with a draw-knife, but if
a bench-vise is to be had, by all means clamp the block in
it and you can work to a much better advantage.

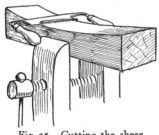

Fig. 35.   Cutting the sheer
in a vise

The draw-knife is by far the
most efficient tool to use for this
part of the work. You will have
so much better control than over
a chisel and can get the weight
of your body to help your muscles do the cutting. If you cannot get one then saw-cut down
vertically across the block to the
line on each side, doing this at intervals along the block
and then split the wood off with a chisel. Finish all
smooth and true with a spokeshave or the small thumb
plane shown in Chapter XI among the tools. The plane
levels off the high spots to a true, fair line.

If you have no band-saw, then take a hand saw and
save much cutting by sawing off the bulk of the wood on
the corners at the bow or forward end of the ship where
she comes in to a point.

The after end having such a gradual taper can be cut
better with a draw-knife or chisel.

From now on comes the real modeling of the ship's
hull. To so hold it that it is all free and clear for cutting,
screw a block of wood down on top of the deck, a piece 2
by 3 inches in size and 9 or 10 inches long which, with the
block inverted, can be firmly clamped in the bench-vise
and is the best way of holding it (Fig. 36).

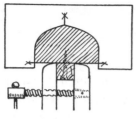

Fig. 36.　Holding the block

Saw off the surplus wood at the bow as shown shaded in Fig. 37. Then with either chisel or drawknife shape the bottom so that it rounds into the shape shown by the midship section mould. Most people unfamiliar with ships make the largest part of their model midway between the ends; but this is seldom the case in real ships and if you measure you will find that the section or mould, which means the same, marked with a symbol at the midship section or largest section in the ship, in our ship is 13 inches from the after end of the deck and only 9⅝ inches from the forward end.

Fig. 37

Mark the location of this section accurately on both sides and also the various other sections as indicated in the plans, for it is at these various points along the model where the moulds must fit to give the required shape to the ship.

Plans of a ship to the average man do not mean anything. They don't convey any idea of what that ship is like. They show a few crooked lines and it takes about 99% imagination to visualize from those curved lines the form of the ship.

We all know the dictionary definition of sections, viz.: "a cutting from" — the act of cutting or dividing. Well, that is all there is to a set of plans of a ship.

If you had one of those pointed-ended loaves of Vienna bread and starting at one end you cut it into thick slices, the first cut would show a small slice, the next larger, and they would become larger and larger until the middle of the loaf was reached and then they would begin to get smaller and smaller again. So would a ship if you cut her into sections the same way. If you laid each slice down on a sheet of paper and with a pencil marked the outline of it around the edge, they would show you how much the loaf of bread increased in bulk between each slice. That is all those mysterious looking sections of the ship are.

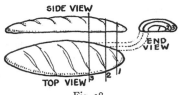

Fig. 38

If it were a square loaf of bread the slices would be nearly all the same size, only a slight diminishing in size on maybe the first thin slice or two, but the shape of the slice off the square loaf of bread is different in shape from that of the Vienna loaf, and as one shows the shape of the Vienna and the other the square loaf, so does a ship cut the same way, show its shape.

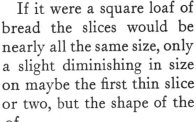

Fig. 39

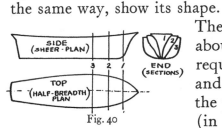

Fig. 40

There is nothing mysterious about any of this, but it does require one to concentrate and use his imagination. In the plans of the "Sea Witch" (in pocket at the end of this volume), she has simply been cut into slices and the edge of each cut shows how she increases or diminishes in size. If we were to cut a slice off her at the section indicated in the forward end (Fig. 41) she would show a shape there corresponding to the shape of the same section marked "S" in the plan of her sections, where all are shown imposed one on top of another.

The same thing is true if she were cut in two at any other section. She would show the same shape that is shown drawn out for that section. So to cut the block to

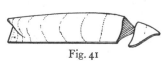

Fig. 41

make it the same shape as the ship, all that we need is a set of patterns giving these section shapes and then to cut the block away until each pattern or mould, as shipbuilders call them, fits exactly at the distance along the ship's hull where these sections were taken from, which is shown by marks at various intervals along the ship, indicated by numbers at the after end and letters at the forward end.

As many men who might care to build this model are not accustomed to measuring with scales where a foot might be represented by only $\frac{1}{8}$ of an inch long, or $\frac{1}{4}$ or $\frac{1}{2}$ of an inch or any size desired, we will give such measurements as will enable anyone with a foot rule, marked into sixteenths of an inch, to lay out the shapes of the moulds needed to model the "Sea Witch."

As both ends are to be cut away we will use the midship frame, marked by a vertical dotted line, as the point of reference and measure from that each way towards the ends.

To lay out a mould for the sweep of the sheer line, and we suggest this be cut out of thin wood rather than paper, as it will hold its shape better, we here give (Fig. 42) the measurements from a straight line square to the sections on which the measurements are measured.

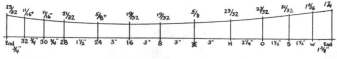

Fig. 42. Sheer mould

Cut a board this shape, retaining the part above the

curved line so that the edge of your mould is convex and not concave, as you will need it to fit down onto the deck as you cut it to see that you get the proper curve.

The shape of the stem is along the rabbet line which is what we are to cut to, and is given by the diagram (Fig. 43), which is carried clear up to where the rail ends.

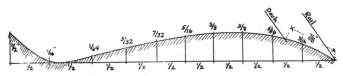

Fig. 43. Mould for shape of stem

At first you will only use this up to where it is marked deck-line, which is ⅞ of an inch measured down along the line below the top of the rail. The actual vertical height of the rail above the deck at this point is only ⅜ of an inch, but measured on the excessive rake forward, which her rabbet line has at this point, we get the ⅞ measurement.

Her stern mould is a series of straight lines and angles, but be careful to get them right to measurements. The top edge is a little higher than the side line of the ship calls for by a scant 1/16 inch, which allows for the round of the deck (Fig. 44). If it were not for the excessive flare at the forward end of our ship one pattern for the deck would be sufficient, but she has such an extreme rake or flare that the deck will be quite some larger, so first make a pattern (Fig. 45) of how the block without

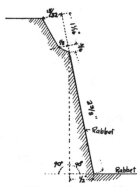

Fig. 44. Stern mould

the ⅛ inch thickness of deck should be shaped and cut your block accordingly — if anything leave the wood a little full and true up this flare in the bow after you have

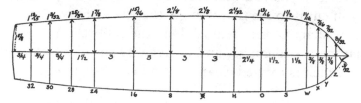

Fig. 45. Mould or pattern for hull below the deck

added the thickness of the deck to it.

The pattern for the deck will be as follows:—

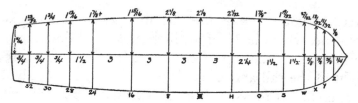

Fig. 46. Pattern for the deck

These deck and top of hull patterns could be cut out of stiff cardboard.

The moulds for the sections are reproduced by the same process — setting off a series of measurements at regular interval. These are what shipbuilders term "off-sets," each measurement in turn being *set off* at its given distance from some straight line — such as the center line of the ship.

The midship mould (indicated on the plans by the vertical dotted line), measuring out from the center of the ship at intervals of ¼ inch up from the rabbet line, gives us the following (Fig. 47):—

This is the shape of one-half of the side of the ship at the widest part.

If you want both sides of the ship all that is necessary

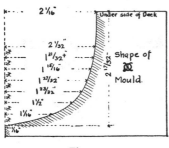

Fig. 47

is to set the same measurements off on the left side of the vertical center line. You will find it much better, however, to work the shape of your model by using half moulds.

Draw each mould out carefully to shape and cut them out with a sharp pointed penknife. In taking off measurements there are occasions where they come a 64th of an inch full or scant and that is why the + or — signs are put after some figures. Others vary even less, so after you have measured off the distances given, make the line connecting them a fair curve even if you have to shave the measurements a little at one side. We are not working with a magnifying glass and micrometer calipers, but only with a two foot rule.

These moulds are merely aids to help you obtain the correct form for your ship model, but you must watch it and see that the whole is a fair-lined, perfect ship when done.

Where the grain of the wood is parallel to the shape, as it is amidship, truer shaping can be done by using a small plane and cutting away gradually until the mould almost fits and then finishing with sandpaper.

It is better to first rough-out the whole model, leaving it an eighth or a sixteenth of an inch full all over, than to try to make a perfect fit of the first mould you cut to and then start and slowly work the shape out true to each mould. A wood rasp or coarse file that is flat on one face and slightly rounded on the other will be found to be a tool of great help in the finishing process. It levels off all the little ridges that are apt to be left in cutting with a chisel or gouge. Sandpaper comes next, about grade No.

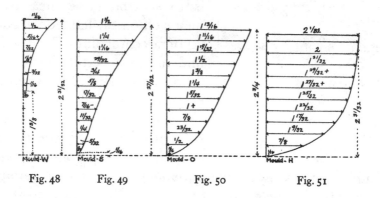

Fig. 48   Fig. 49   Fig. 50   Fig. 51

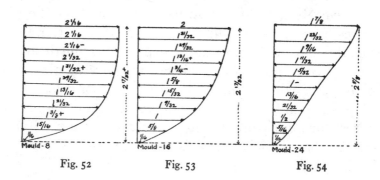

Fig. 52   Fig. 53   Fig. 54

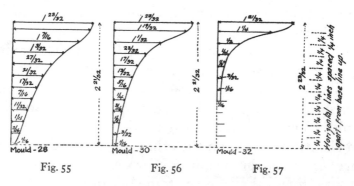

Fig. 55   Fig. 56   Fig. 57

SECTIONAL MOULDS — "SEA WITCH"

1, and then when all is fair, smooth off for painting with sandpaper No. 0.

For a space of 1/16 of an inch on each side of the center line wood must be left uncut along the bottom and up each end to receive the keel stem and stern post.

Some men prefer to work with moulds that show both sides of the ship as shown in the preceding sketches and while they have some advantage over the half mould in that when you apply them you have a sheer or deck height mark on two sides to give you a check on whether the model is true on each side, yet they are rather clumsy to work with, require more cardboard being left around them to insure their holding their true shape and, what is the greatest drawback, require modeling both sides at once.

I find it far more convenient to work with half moulds (Fig. 58) — that is only one side at a time. Then you can devote all your time to getting one side fair before starting to model the other. The only precaution necessary is to be sure that the center-line of the mould coincides with the center-line on the hull and is applied squarely to it. In the ends, particularly where the levels are rank, a slight shift in the mould will make the hull either too fine or too full. Along in the middle part of the ship, where the shape is rounded, it is easily cut with chisel and small plane, but it gets more difficult towards the ends where you have to cut more across the grain and the ends become hollowed. There you will have to use a gouge, a wide, flat one, or the small plane shown in Chapter XI, with its gouge-

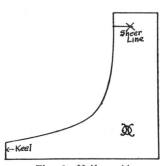

Fig. 58. Half mould

shaped blade, to cut the hollow down at the fore-foot.
Aft is by far the hardest part
of all to shape, as the hollow
gets more and more acute as
you go aft to the stern post
and you will need smaller and
smaller gouges to cut it.

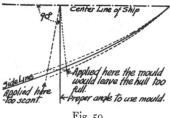

Fig. 59

Do not try to hurry this part of the work; be careful,
for the beauty of the model depends upon getting this
part of the ship, its "run" as sailors term it, fair and true.

Use a small strip of wood as a batten and bend it over
the hull fore and aft along in the run and you can soon
see where the humps and hollows are. Here again the
round back of a file works well to assist in fairing up the
model as it irons out local unevennesses. It is better than
a wood cutting tool which will cut deeper when it comes
to the softer streaks of wood than it does on the hard
annular rings that are more or less prominent in all
woods. It is the absence of these and the uniform even
grain that makes the Michigan cork pine so desirable for
modeling and pitch pine so totally unfit.

The transoms, at the stern, look simple enough, yet
they are more often modeled wrong through not understanding the principles on which they are laid out. From
the days of the old Spanish galleons down to the days of

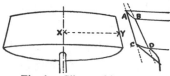

Fig. 60. Clipper ship transom

the clipper ships the same rules
have been adhered to. There
are few flat surfaces in a ship.
Nearly every piece of wood has
a curve one way or another.
So while the transom looks flat to the eye it really has a
slight curve worked in it (Fig. 60). In the distance represented by X-Y the face of the clipper ship's transom

curves at the top the amount
shown between A and B, and
at the bottom the distance
C-D, which is a trifle greater.
The radial lines all converging
at a point above the stern (Fig.
61) will explain the theory bet-

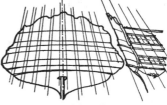

Fig. 61. Spanish galleon transom

ter than words. It gives symmetry and grace, the result
of years of evolution in shipbuilding. So in cutting the
face of the transom on your model ship remember this
and shape it accordingly and she will not have the ungainly, unship-like appearance so often seen in models.

Very often after the model is all shaped, if it is left for
an hour or two so as to rest your eyes from the continual
close scrutiny you have been giving it, you can see at a
glance some slight unfairness to be filed down. So don't
be in too great a hurry to push the work on. Be sure it is
fair and true before you unscrew it from the block.

Then you are ready to hollow it out. I generally hollow all my models out so that the wood is approximately
half an inch thick, but this is not necessary and digging
them out with a gouge requires great care that the gouge
doesn't slip and cut your hand for you can't clamp the
hull tight enough in a vise to hold it without a possibility
of cracking it. Boring holes to help split out the wood as
you come to it helps somewhat, but the greatest safe-
guard of all is to have a good sharp tool that will cut as
you intend. The dull one that picks up a shred of wood
and slips suddenly is a dangerous tool to work with.
Keep your oil stones handy and slick up the tools occasionally as you use them and they will not get dull.

If you cut too deep in any place, or if, as it sometimes
happens, a bad spot develops in the wood caused by some
bruise when the tree was young, and which afterwards

grew over and became entirely covered on the outside, you can remedy this by putting in "a Dutchman." Chisel down about an eighth of an inch so as to avoid shim edges and set in with glue a piece of wood matching the run of the grain as true as you can and then you have new wood on which to continue modeling.

FISHING SCHOONER

CHAPTER IV

The Deck

WE are now ready to put on the deck, for which we have allowed ⅛ inch thickness, but we make the deck out of ¼ inch thick pine for the reason that all decks have a camber or crown which makes the water drain off to the edges into gutters, where it is allowed to run overboard through lead pipes set flush in the deck and going out through the ship's side about a

Fig. 62. Hull ready for deck

foot below the deck line. For the deck you will need a piece of white pine 24 inches long, 4½ inches wide and ¼ inch thick. Lay it on top of the model and mark out the ship's shape. Then cut it out, not quite to this line. Have it about an eighth of an inch full all around, except around the bows, where, owing to the flare of the ship, you need all of a quarter of an inch of wood left.

Mark a line or scratch-gauge the ⅛ inch thickness the deck edge is to finish to and plane the top of the board so that it makes a true arc of a circle across from side to side all the way from the stern to within six inches of the bow where the thickness of the board tapers down to ⅛ of an inch, the crown of the deck gradually diminishing towards the point at the bow.

Sandpaper down to a smooth surface and after ruling a light center line down the middle with lead pencil, set off spots near each end by which to lay out the seams of the deck planks. These should be spaced every 3/32 of an inch apart, and with a straight-edge and sharp pointed awl scratched in so that the deck looks as if it were really laid in narrow planks. Be careful that the awl's point does not run off, following the grain of the wood instead of the straight-edge, as it is apt to.

Now take a tube of raw umber, the kind that comes ready mixed with oil, and squeeze out enough to coat one side of this deck. Thin it with turpentine and add a few drops of Japan drier, giving the deck a good even coat of this and working it well down into the scratch marks and after letting it stand about five minutes, take a rag and rub it all off. Rub hard, so that you practically bare the wood again, and at the same time fill the seams so that they look just like the pitch-filled deck seams of a real ship and the wood takes on a slightly oiled and shaded appearance resembling wood that has seen some sea service. Don't try to make your ship have that 100% perfect look of a toy ship, as many affect. Try to make it appear as ships look. That is why raw umber is far preferable to that jet black, shoe polish look that never existed in any real ship, but only in people's imagination.

See that the deck makes a perfect joint when bent down on the hull. If it does not, take a full-sized sheet of sandpaper and lay it between the deck and the hull, sand side next to the uneven places on the hull and pressing on the deck, and then work the sandpaper back and forth, just an inch or so, and a perfect joint can be made very quickly. Then spread glue on the edge of the hull. Nail it fast every three-quarters of an inch or so with small ½ inch to ⅝ inch bung-headed brads. Use steel ones. Brass does not hold well.

Punch the nail heads just a trifle below the surface of the wood. Then with the little iron plane smooth the deck edge down around the edges flush with the

Fig. 63. Edge of the deck

rest of the hull, carrying out the flare of the bows just as the hull gives you the slant.

There is a reason for using a deck ¼ inch thick instead of ⅛ inch. It does away with fitting several deck beams across the hull to give the necessary crown to the ⅛ inch deck, but what is of more importance, it gives wood enough to hold such deck fittings as the hatch-combings and bitts around each mast, which, on a thin deck, always become loose and cause no end of trouble later when you cannot get at them to replace them.

To make the quarter-deck, that raised deck at the stern end of the ship sacred to the use of the officers only, except when necessary for the common sailors to use it in working the ship's gear and for the man at the steering wheel, a piece of pine is needed 6 inches long, 4 inches wide and a stout half an inch in thickness.

Shape out to the under side so that it fits perfectly around the edges. Here, again, after you have gouged and planed the shape as nearly as possible, the sandpaper can be laid on, this time the sand side up, and by rubbing the block forming the poop deck forward and backward a perfect fit is assured if it is kept pressed down. Glue and then brad this on securely and finish its surface with the same crown as the deck which will reduce the height at the side to 13/32 of an inch, and then crease to imitate planks and paint the same as was done with the main deck. Shape the sides to fit the templates and give the stern the same slant as that below it.

Fig. 64. The quarter deck

Be careful to get the sides on a true, fair curve at the deck edges, with about 1/16 of an inch narrowing in at the top on each side.

There is one more block to put on the deck forward

before the more delicate work begins and that is what forms the forecastle head. Owing to her excessive flare at the bows, the "Sea Witch" had more than any other ship ever built, and the fastenings to hold on this forecastle head will require considerable care so that they do not come out through the ship's side below. Keep them slanted well inboard.

As the bowsprit comes in forward, make the two sides of the forecastle head separate. It requires two pieces seven inches long, 1½ inches wide and ½ inch thick. Nail one side on at a time, temporarily, and cut the outside shape according to the moulds; but you will have to do considerable shaping here by the eye, as the flare is so extreme and the bevels so rank. The shape given for the deck of the forecastle head is the best guide you have to go by. Keep to that shape and you are sure to preserve the flare that gives this ship her character.

As the space under the forecastle head was open, only enough wood to represent the paint lockers, etc., that were usually built against the ship's side just under the deck edge, can be left. From these, aft, the bulwarks must be carved out of these side pieces to a ½ inch thickness far enough back to reach a point where the bulwarks were about vertical.

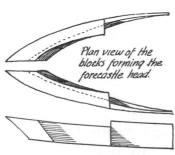

Plan view of the blocks forming the forecastle head.

Fig. 65. The forecastle head

For a deck a piece of pine ⅛ inch thick and four inches long by four inches wide will do. From a point ⅛ of an inch aft of the heavy jog in the blocks for the forecastle head, cut them both down in height, so that this deck will come flush with the part left standing aft.

Then glue them down and nail fast, being careful to have both sides alike. On a real ship the bowsprit can be taken out and put in again, but as we are not small enough to get under the forecastle head and let go the fastenings we must put the bowsprit in before the deck goes on and to prevent this important spar from breaking, it is a wise precaution to make it out of some hard wood, such as oak or ash. The bowsprit should be made six inches long and ¼ inch square and to get the proper angle of rise or steeve cut the bottom edge, beginning 1¾ inches from the end, to nothing at the top edge (Fig. 66). Glue and nail this fast to the deck, snug between the blocks of the forecastle head, and then you can fasten on the deck of the forecastle head, creasing the plank seams and painting it the same as the other decks were done to make the deck seams show plainly.

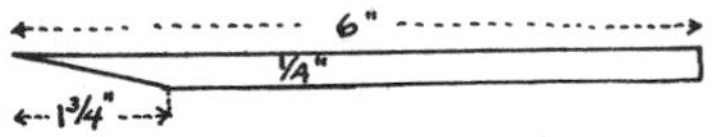

Fig. 66. The bowsprit

The keel, stem and stern-post are all the same thickness, ⅛ of an inch. The keel is a parallel strip 3/16 of an inch deep. The stern post tapers and the stem requires a piece a little over a half an inch in width in order to cut out its S-shaped curves. For about 2½ inches forward the rabbet line, to which we have modeled our ship, rises slightly above a straight keel line. This can be built in with a slim, wedge-shaped piece and trimmed off flush on the sides with the keel.

While in the real ship the joint between the stern and the keel would be in the form of a hook scarph (Fig. 67), all that detail, being covered with paint, is unnecessary work; but to prevent their shifting it is a good plan to

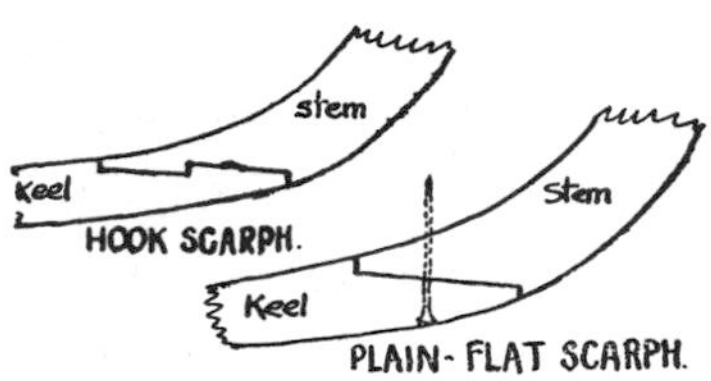

Fig. 67

cut a flat scarph so that one fastening can be put through both, which will assure their staying in perfect alignment. It is the same way aft, where the sternpost meets the keel. In real ships it is cut with a mortise and tenon joint (Fig. 68), but on account of the liability of such a small piece as is left at the end splitting off, it is a better practice in models to bevel the end (Fig. 69), which prevents its working back and also makes it stronger.

In fastening all these pieces, and also in putting on the deck, it is a wise precaution to bore for the fastenings so that you do not split the wood. Use the little pin-vise and drills from number 65 to 70, according to the size of the nails or pins that you use. I generally use a 65 drill and small steel brads for this part and a number 70 drill where pins are used. Buy a box of small, short, bank pins, for you will need many of them before the model is completed.

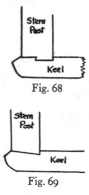

Fig. 68

Fig. 69

In building the bulwarks we come to the first small, delicate job. If this is your first attempt, I would suggest that you make these out of one piece of wood ⅛ of an inch thick, one inch wide and sixteen inches long. This bulwark is to extend from the poop deck aft, forward to the forecastle head. Use your small iron plane and fit the lower edge to the slight sweep or curve in the deck fore and aft and have the bulwark inclined inboard just a little, except forward, where it has to twist so that the top edge flares outboard to fair in with the sweep of the forecastle head. Notch the after end into the block, forming the quarter-deck, for about ¾ of an inch and glue and nail it fast to it. The forward end can be cut on a slant so that it laps up on the thin after end of the forecastle block that was cut down to the bulwarks' thickness

and held with one nail that
goes down through both parts
(Fig. 70). With ⅛ of an inch
of wood you can edge-nail it

Fig. 70. Bulwark joint

down into the deck and hull with ordinary pins, cutting
off their heads and driving
them down flush at intervals
of about an inch. If the bulwarks have not been sized
down to a parallel depth of
13/32 inch, and it is better

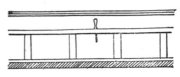

Fig. 71. Bulwark stanchions

not to do so until they are fastened on, take your small
plane and work them down now to that depth, fairing out
with the height of the quarter-deck, so that they make a
fair, unbroken sweep from bow to stern.

A far more difficult way, but one which, by its appearance when completed, compensates for the trouble taken,

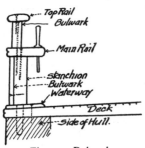

Fig. 72. Bulwarks

is to build up the bulwarks so that
the little stanchions or timber-
heads show, which was the usual
open rail or merchant ship construction (Figs. 71 and 72). Men-
of-war generally had their bulwarks sheathed up inside as well
as planked outside — frigate built
as it was called — which made the

bulwarks much thicker, thereby offering greater resist-
ance to small shot and protecting the crew on her deck.

This style of construction necessitates putting in the
waterways, or raised pieces of deck along the sides, before
the stanchions and bulwarks are put up. This requires a
very thin strip, only 1/16 of an inch thick, shaped so that
it runs parallel with the side of the ship and extends in
from the edge ¼ of an inch. But on account of the curva-

ture to the side forward, unless you work a short piece forward to take care of it there, a piece about an inch in width will be needed.   Round off the sharp corner on the

Fig. 73.   Waterways bored for timber heads

inner, upper edge of this piece and glue and tack it down securely to the deck with bank pins, filing their heads off flush, with a smoothing file, after it is tacked fast.   Be careful to keep these pins out of the way of where you have to bore for the stanchions or timber heads, which is every ½ inch from the poop deck to forecastle head, the center of the holes being a full ⅛ of an inch back from the edge.   Measure these spots off and with a drill a trifle under ⅛ of an inch in diameter bore vertical holes (Fig. 73), taking great care to have them slant back or inboard at the top just a little, not quite 1/16 of an inch in ½ of an inch of height, to match the poop deck's slight narrowing in at the top.   To match the flare of the side forward, these holes, at the forward end, must gradually become vertical and then begin to flare until the last one matches the flare of the bulwark at the forecastle head.

Give the waterways a coat of paint.   Rub this down lightly with No. oo sandpaper and when dry give them a second coat.

In the meantime you can be making a few strips of pine ⅛ of an inch square and long enough to make forty-eight pieces ¾ of an inch in length and paint these white

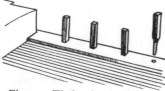

Fig. 74.   Timber heads dipped in glue and driven into holes

on three sides only, leaving one side bare to take glue, from which the stanchions or timber heads are to be cut.   With a penknife, round off the ends of these stanchions and cut into

¾ of an inch lengths so that they fit snug in the holes drilled in the waterways. Give the peg end of each just a slight touch of glue and drive them into the holes. Too much glue bubbles out and hardens into an unsightly fillet in the corner. If any such appears wipe or scrape it away.

You now have a ledge 1/16 of an inch between these stanchions and the edge of your ship for the bulwarks. Notch the after end into the block forming the poop deck and forward, instead of lapping it on top of the forecastle head piece, it will also have to be let in flush on the outside sufficient to hold it with glue and the points of a few bank pins cut off short with cutting pliers.

Put a little glue on the outer edge of each stanchion as you put these bulwarks on in order to help hold it in position and also use the points, only about ⅛ of an inch long, of a few bank pins, to fasten an occasional stanchion.

The tops of the stanchions will stand at irregular heights above the bulwark, which latter should be shaped as true as possible to its required height of 13/64 of an inch as it is very delicate work trying to shape it down later.

The best thing I have found to cut off the stanchions even with the top of the bulwark is a pair of end-cutting pliers kept well sharpened. You can quickly snip them off (Fig. 75) with these and do any trueing-up necessary with either a very sharp penknife or a fine, flat file.

When they are all leveled off in a true sweep from forecastle head to poop, they are ready for the main rail. Paint the inside of the bulwarks while they are easy to get at and give the waterways and stanchions their final coat of white as you cannot very well

Fig. 75

get a paint brush up under the rail after that goes on.

From the foremast, aft, the "Sea Witch" is so straight that her rail can be made in a straight piece for each side, ⅛ of an inch by ⅜ of an inch, sixteen inches long; and what little curve there is can be bent into it. Paint both edges and the top with white, but leave the underside bare, as glue gets a more permanent hold on bare wood. Then glue coat the underside and starting aft, where it lays flat on the poop deck, nail it down with bank pins so that its edge projects 1/16 of an inch beyond the side of the ship. From the poop, forward, considerable care is needed. Bore through the rail and for about 1/16 of an inch down, into the end of every fourth stanchion and using only the ends of bank pins, nail the rail to assist the glue in holding it fast into its place, which is with a projection of 1/16 of an inch to form a molding beyond the side. Be sure that this extends out evenly, all along, for accuracy in such details makes or spoils a model's appearance. If it sticks out too far, anywhere, upon a critical examination after the glue has set, work it down even with a flat file or sandpaper.

Where this rail becomes too stiff to bend in conformity with the sweep of the ship's side, take a wide enough piece of 1/16 inch pine to cut the shape out and piece out the forward end in that manner, nailing it down flat on the forecastle head the same as on the poop deck aft.

Across the stern fit a piece of waterway, 5/16 of an inch wide from side to side, and at the forward end of the poop and after end of the forecastle head fit similar narrower pieces — ¼ of an inch in width is sufficient, and put on so that the inner edges project a very little — say a 32d of an inch.

In fitting all such pieces it is a good plan to cut their ends on a slight bevel so that the under part is a trifle

longer than the top. They
can be put in by a slight
springing up of the middle

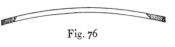

Fig. 76

and when once glued and fastened with pin points it holds
down better.

Another piece of bulwark stuff ⅛ of an inch thick and
finished to a height of 7/32 of an inch above the main
rail, now has to be put on from end to end and across the
stern (Fig. 76). "Flare" or "flam," is any part of the
ship's hull that extends out away from the center of the
ship as it goes up. "Tumble home," is that part which
gets narrower or slants in towards the center line of the
ship as it goes up from the water.

This bulwark at the after end "tumbles home" slightly,
comes plumb just aft of the foremast and then rolls over
into a strong flare around the bows. You will have to cut
the forward end out a solid piece just as you did for the
bulwark below, finishing it down to only ⅛ of an inch in
thickness; and due to the slight twist in the bulwark aft,
it will lay on easier if shaped slightly, fore and aft, and
fitted a true fit before fastening, instead of trying to force
the twist in and hold it down with the fastenings, because
you have so very little under it to fasten into. Only the
heads of the stanchions are fit to drive the pin points into
and then it requires considerable care to keep them from
splitting.

Use a very fine drill, No. 76 or even No. 80, which is
about as thick as a hair, and first drill a hole and then the
pin will follow and not run out as it is apt to do if there
is no small hole to guide it. You have better control over
the drill and can keep it true into the end of the stanchion.

If you cannot get drills fine enough, then take needles,
for they answer nearly as well and do not break so easily.

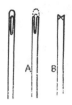

Fig. 77

Break the eye off so that you have the two sides left (as shown in Fig. 77a), then rub on a fine emery stone so that you sharpen the sides of the eye with one side slanting one way, and the other the opposite (as shown in Fig. 77b) and you will have a quick-cutting drill for fine work. You can snip the needle off with cutting pliers. A tool I have found most useful for similar work is a crochet needle; a very fine one with the point ground down so that the hook on the end disappears and you will have a fine brad awl that by twisting between your fingers you can drill small holes very accurately.

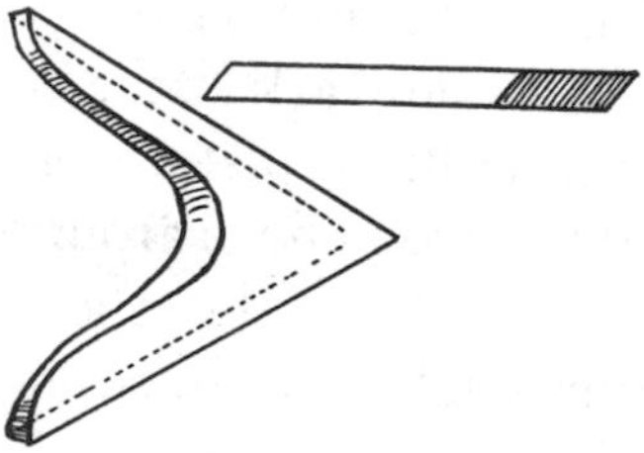

To stiffen the bulwarks where they meet forward, shape out a little throat knee (Fig. 78) to fit snug in the angle they make and after gluing the underside and V-shaped ends, tack it down into the forecastle head deck

Fig. 78.   Knee to hold bulwarks forward

and this gives you something into which you can nail to hold the ends of the bulwarks snug.

For fastenings where the wood to be held is thin and also soft, hold a bank pin snug up near its head with a pair of pincers and then file the round part of the pin head down to a very thin, flat head. When the model is painted such a fastening will not show. Cut the pin off to a length that will stay buried and not come out through the knee and then file it down to a sharp point again.

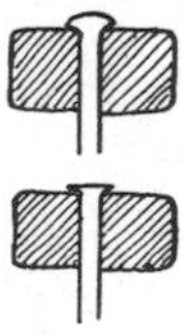

Fig.79. Pin-head filed down flat

To hold the bulwarks at the after end of the poop, cut two little knees to fit the angle of "tumble home," required for the side, with its after arm to the slant of the transom. Glue and nail this down securely onto the waterways of the poop deck and you will have wood enough to securely fasten this corner and to hold the piece across the transom end.

After fairing off the knees and the top of this bulwark put on the finishing piece — the top rail. This is the lightest rail of all so far. It is only 1/16 of an inch thick, 3/16 of an inch wide and it runs from bow to stern. I was fortunate enough to have on hand for this some 1/16 of an inch kiln-dried, aëroplane mahogany, which, on account of its fine grain, made a very handsome rail when finished off in varnish. You want for this work a wood not too prone to split, and that is why, in most cases, where it is to be painted, I prefer a good grade of white pine. You can push the fastenings in without splitting, and glue clings to it well.

Across the stern, make this rail out of heavier stuff and shape it to fit the crown or curve of the deck sweep. Don't try to spring it down and hold the curve by fastenings.

CHAPTER V

The Hull

NOW comes a delicate operation after the outside of the hull has been sandpapered down smooth with No. o or No. oo sandpaper; and that is to cut in the water-line and crease in the planking lines.

I have found the safest way to scratch in the water-line is to mark the height at bow and stern where the water-line is to go. The "Sea Witch's" water-line is two

Fig. 80. The water-line on the hull

inches above the top of her keel forward, and two and a quarter inches aft (Fig. 80).

Mark these distances at the ends and then turn her upside down on a level table-top, blocked up so they are an even distance above the table.

Then plane up a block of wood thick enough so that a sharp pointed piece of steel wire, stapled fast on top of it, will just touch the spot at either end. Be sure she is level, so that both rails touch, for the water-line will be higher on one side than on the other if she is not set perfectly level. Try your improvised scratch awl to see that it is going to come an even distance down on each side, before you start to scratch in the water-line (Fig. 81).

Your scratch awl must extend two and a half inches beyond the block in order to reach in at the ends where the shape of the hull slopes back, and you should be certain that the scratch awl and the bottom of the block are parallel to each other.

Fig. 81. Marking the water-line

48

With the model set true and level it is an easy matter to scratch a level line around the hull, but be careful to hold the block, on which the scratch awl is fastened, down flat on the top of the table and watch out that the

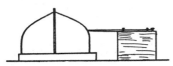

Fig. 82. Marking the water-line

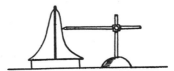

Fig. 83. Marking the water-line

point does not run up or down following the grain of the wood. It requires care and easy scratching. Don't press too hard against the hull or the sharp point of the awl will try to follow the softer layers of grain in the wood.

Metal workers have a tool called a surface gauge (Fig. 84), a flat, base-piece made heavy so that it lies flat, with an upright shaft and across it an arm that slides up and down the shaft and can be locked fast by means of a set-screw to any desired height. By attaching a pencil point to the end of this arm the water-line can be marked with accuracy around the hull of the model.

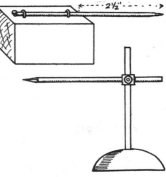

Fig. 84. Surface gauges

This line represents the top of her copper which, being laid on over sheet felt, hides her planking lines from here down to the keel and this part is to be painted a dull, yellowish brown. Yellow ochre and brown with just a drop of red makes a good color imitating copper, particularly after it dries out well.

To scratch in the lines of the planking is not an easy

job. Ships' planks are not, as most people suppose, parallel boards put on like the boards on a house, only, of course, without the lap. They are like the staves of a barrel, big in the middle and taper in width at each end.

The upper part of the bulwark, between the top rail and the main rail, can be creased to represent three parallel boards.

From the main rail down to the main deck, rule into six planks up as far as the part where the bow rounds in. From there forward you will find the interval between rail and deck, when spaced off on the excessive bevel found there, is a much greater distance than it is in the mid-length of the ship. Here the shipbuilder widens the planks, where the bevel is the greatest, to prevent the planks from having too great a sny or crook to them and to make the planking lines show a true, fair curve instead of a hump like a camel's back, as they would if carried along in evenly-spaced widths. Each plank is narrowed down at the bow to about two-thirds of what it is amidships (Fig. 85). This makes them assume a fan-like appearance just above the copper-line at the bow.

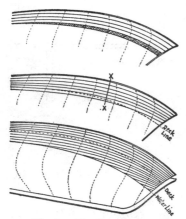

Fig. 85. Planking the hull

To more clearly understand why this appearance should be, look at the difference in the girth of frame X and frame Y in the accompanying diagram (Fig. 86). Measure the length around each of these on a strip of paper, then divide these lengths into halves and then quarters and space them back around the frames. That is the principle upon which

ships' planks are laid out and
you can readily see why they
slant up so at the rabbet at the
stern; and the difference in
widths of the planking lines A, B
and C at the middle of the ship
(Fig. 86) and at the bow shows
how much each plank must taper

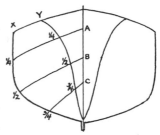

Fig. 86. The taper on planking

proportionately as its width is
to the whole space to be
planked. On the sharp turn to
the quarters aft, the same effect
is shown, the planks being only
one-half as wide at their ends
and then widening out when

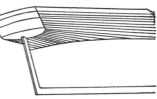

Fig. 87. Planking under the quarters

they get under the counter of the ship again (Fig. 87).

Be careful under the counter, for much taper there will
make the planking lines back towards the center of the
ship, as shown in Fig. 88, which is decidedly wrong. I
would advise one to lay out
the planking with pencil lines,
the first time he tries this part
of the work, and to get them all
to run in true, fair curves before they are scratched in per-
manently, otherwise he may
nearly ruin the appearance of
his model.

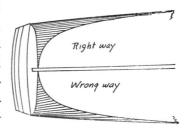

Fig. 88. Planking under the counter

The ease or difficulty one experiences in creasing in the
lines varies with the evenness of the grain of wood from
which the model is cut. Along the flat of the side it is
easy, but when crossing the hard, annular rings, denoting
the tree's yearly growth, it is sometimes very hard to
make an even depth of seam between the planks. A

scratch awl will not make any impression on this hard wood. I have a file, one of a set called "die sinkers," that has a knife-like blade with teeth on the thin edge, that cuts creases across these ridges.

Crease horizontally across the stern the same way, for the transom is planked across with narrow planks the same way as the sides (Fig. 89). The seam between the sides and stern planking some builders made right in the

corner, but more often the side planks were carried aft, their ends showing around the edge of the transom. Some sort of hard rubber, celluloid or other

Fig. 89. Planking on the transom

flexible rule is required to hold along the line to be creased, to guide the awl point; but be careful that you don't make the seams a succession of straight lines forming angles where they meet, instead of a fair, sweeping line from end to end.

Take pains to do a neat job and the appearance of your model when completed will amply repay you, but it might better be left uncreased than done in a careless manner, for small as this detail of the ship may seem it either makes or spoils its appearance.

Builders and ship captains used to take great pride in their ships and the fair sweetness of her planking lines was one of the first points they looked for to criticise or to admire as the case might be.

Ships were always insured and Lloyds of England did the bulk of this among English speaking people. France had its Bureau Veritas, etc., and in later years America started the American Bureau of Shipping. These companies issued set rules directing how the various sized ships should be constructed and then graded them accordingly. They required a certain thickness of plank-

ing and one of their rules insisted on extra thick planking for the wales, as the planking just under the deck
edge is termed.

In the Lloyds' rules of 1870, the wales for a 900 ton
ship were required to be 5½ inches thick, while the rest
of the side planking below it was only 4¼ inches thick;
and the depth of these wales, for it included a belt composed of several planks, was, to quote the rule, "When
the extreme length of the ship measured from the fore
part of the stem to the after part of the stern post on the
range of upper deck, is six times her depth of hold (and
under) the wales are to be in breadth 3 inches to every
foot of the depth of hold."

The "Sea Witch's" depth of hold was 19 feet, 0 inches.
So 3 inches multiplied 19 times gives us 57 inches or 4
feet, 9 inches, just under ⅝ of an inch on our model, of
thick wale strakes. Measure this down a scant ⅝ inch,
on the sides below her deck, and diminish it at the ends
as the planks tapered fore and aft.

This line, generally indicated by a heavy shadow, you
see indicated on most old plans and paintings of ships
and it makes a very effective finish on a model to cut

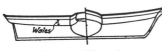

Fig. 90. The wales

down a scant 1/32 of an inch
below this line so that the
wales show raised a little as in
the real ship. They end aft,
just on the corner formed by the sharp turn of the bilge
at the transom.

Right at the extreme forward end, where they fit into
the rabbet of the stem, these planks are thinned down to
the same thickness as the rest of the planking, so this
ridge dies out to nothing in the last inch or so. American
Bureau of Shipping rules call for even thicker wales. A
900 ton ship requires 5 inch wales to 3½ inch side plank-

ing, so a decided ridge or difference in thickness is quite permissible.

Give the topsides, from the water-line to the rail, a coat of raw umber, working it well into the seams of the planking to make them show prominently as they will, if, after the paint has set but not dried hard, you take a cloth and rub her down hard. Don't be afraid if a lot of the paint does come off on the rag. She is to have three or four coats before she is finished.

FISHING SCHOONER, ABOUT 1800

CHAPTER VI

THE RUDDER AND TRANSOM

BEFORE we put on the deck furniture let us make and hang the rudder and then all the bottom is ready to work up to the final painting.

Ships' rudders were always very narrow; necessarily so, for the leverage is very great. Even on one only three feet wide, as on the "Sea Witch," which was 170 feet long, many times when she was carrying a press of sail, as she swooped along over the big ocean swells — and there are seas, when you get off soundings, that make a ship of her size look mighty small indeed — it required all of two men's strength to hold the steering wheel to prevent it from getting away from them and spinning around like a buzz saw. I know only too well, for, coming home in the bark "James A. Wright," off Cape Horn, I was assisting the man whose trick it was at the wheel, and once, when she took a wild swoop on the crest of a grey-back, Joe let go the wheel unexpectedly. My sticky, oilskin coat wrapped around one spoke of the wheel that was suddenly wrenched from my grip and I was catapulted clear over the wheel and landed on my head on the weather side with one arm disabled for three days. That rudder was large enough, just then.

Cut the rudder, the shape shown, out of 3/16 inch white pine and bore a hole for the rudder head to go up about a quarter of an inch into the hull. To get this hole so that its center line lines up with the afterside of the stern-post requires the top of the stern-post being dug out with a small gouge, half the thickness of the rudder stock, so that the pintles and gudgeons — those little hinges or hooks and eyes as we make them—will all line up true and give you room to work the drill up into the hull. Bore slowly until you have the hole well started or you may split out the little cross-grained wood aft of the bit.

The "Sea Witch" had a modern rudder, a "plug-stock" rudder as it is called, to distinguish it from the older type

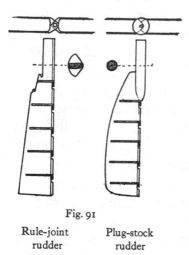

Fig. 91

Rule-joint rudder   Plug-stock rudder

of rule-joint rudder so universally used before the year 1800. The rule-joint rudder (Fig. 91) had its hinge point on the forward edge of the rudder and the rudder stock or head carried straight up. Where it entered the transom a V-shaped hole had to be left to give it room to swing from side to side, having an opening where much water could get in, but this was prevented by a rudder coat of heavy canvas painted and nailed to both the rudder and the transom above it, with enough bagginess or slack cloth to permit the turning of the rudder, and yet to keep out the water. With the plug-stock rudder (Fig. 91), the rudder stock centered over the pintles below, but half the stock's thickness was shaped forward of this

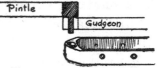

Fig. 92. Pintle and gudgeon

center line of the pintles so that a round stock turned in a snug-fitting, circular rudder port in the transom of the ship and no water could get in. All rudder ports of course were made like a water-tight box inside.

The round rudder stock after extending down out of the stern of the ship, far enough to permit enough bolts being put through it to hold securely the back of the rudder or blade, was tapered down to a point at the first pintle and fitted snugly into a grooved section at the top of the stern-post shaped to receive it (Fig. 93). The edges of both stern-post and rudder were chamfered slightly from there down, so their faces would just touch when the rudder swung 30 degrees each side of the centre.

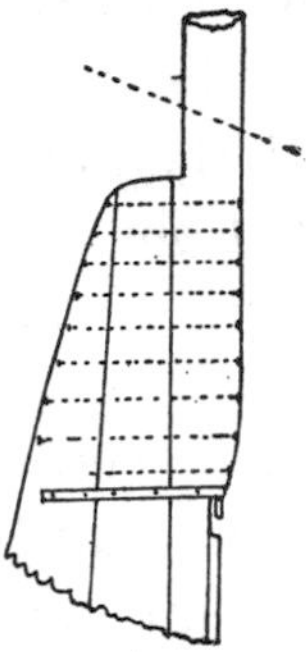

Fig. 93

There should be at least five sets of rudder braces, as the pintles and gudgeons are termed (Figs. 91 and 92). The first, right at the point of the plug, the others equally spaced below. Our model is rather small to make up sets of braces. Some men imitate them by gluing on thin, narrow strips of paper, as that is about as thick as they would be according to scale. When this is done, remember that the Lloyds' rule demands that the gudgeon straps on the hull must extend back far enough to get two bolts through the planking. In our model the braces will space about one-half an inch apart and they can be made of bank pins. Hold the head end of the pin in a flame for a few seconds to anneal or soften the brass of which it is made or it may break off when you bend it.

Make five with eyes in their ends, bending them with the sharp pointed end of round nosed pliers, so small that another pin will just fit snugly into the eye and make four where ⅛ of an inch of the end is bent at right angles to the pin (Fig. 94). Be sure the eyes are centered with the shaft of the pin and not bent on one side of it only. You have to kink the eye back after it is formed to get this just right.

Fig. 94

Put the five eyes in the stern and then slip the rudder into place and mark accurately where to put the hooks or pintles so that they will all hook equally into these eyes.

To prevent any "throw" to the rudder, as it is turned from side to side, the pintles should be directly under the center of the rudder stock above it in the hole in the ship's stern. This brings the pins or pintles flush with the wood on the forward edge of the rudder, so cut out shallow notches to permit the eye hooking behind the pin in the rudder as shown in Figure 95.

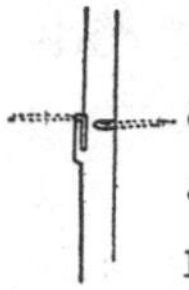

If our model were larger we could show to better advantage some interesting rudder details — such as the wood-lock and dumb-brace. As some may make large models, we will explain this.

Fig. 95   The dumb-brace is generally below water and few men, unless they have seen wooden ships built or hauled out, would notice that under the point of the third pintle down from the top, a metal shoulder is fitted so that the weight of the rudder wears on the end of this pintle and so does not grind the adjoining edges of pintles and gudgeons (Fig. 96). There is practically no weight to the rudder when the ship is loaded down as it about floats its own weight when well submerged. But ships often have to make voyages in ballast, that is with no cargo, instead of which anything heavy, such as sand, rock, old junk of any kind obtainable, is put into her to give her stability enough to carry sail.

The wood-lock is put in to prevent the rudder from unshipping as it might in a heavy sea with the ship loaded deep in the water.

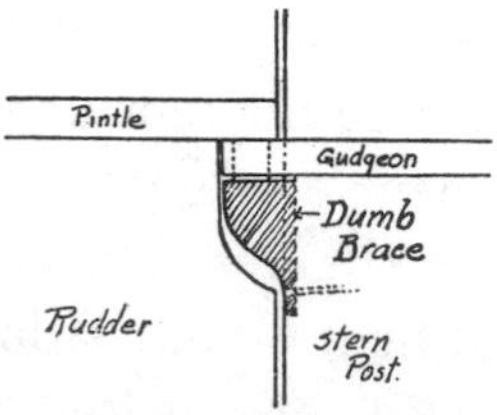

The wood-lock consists of a section cut out of the rudder, just under the second pintle, wide enough on one side so that with the rudder turned, this wedge-

Fig. 96. Dumb brace

shaped block can be put in and bolted. Being fitted snug up to the pintle it prevents the pintles lifting up out of the gudgeons (Fig. 97).

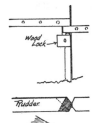

The drift bolt which holds it in place can always be got at to back it out for the purpose of unshipping the rudder. Some men will not care to go into all this detail, but a model should be instructive to those who come along in the future and show as much detail as it is possible to convey in the size of the model. The majority of model builders are quite satisfied if they can make something that looks like a ship;

Fig. 97. Wood lock

but the reason for this I have found to be largely due to lack of explanation and illustration of the various details than to lack of desire to do so on the part of the model builders. From childhood I have eagerly studied details of ships, but not until I built them myself and went to sea on them could I find much needed detail for model making. What has been published is scattered in fragments through so many different volumes it is almost impossible to collect all in any concise form for reference. Many interesting facts are hidden away in narratives undetected except by those who know enough about ships to recognize them and to separate the fact from its camouflage of technicality.

Before we leave the rudder let us finish it off with its rudder chains. Bend another bank pin into an eye and push it into the after edge of the rudder, just above the water-line, leaving it sticking out about 3/16 of an inch and into this hook two small rudder chains, useful, if the steering gear breaks down, to rig up a jury steering gear to. These chains make fast to two eyes in the transom at the deck level with slack enough to permit the rudder to swing over freely.

The inability of most model makers to secure chains small enough has ruined the appearance of more models than anything else I know of. These chains should be not less than twenty-two links to the inch, which is about the size used on eyeglass holders. Sometimes you can find in five and ten cent stores lorgnettes with this size of chain on them; if not, a jewelers' supply house usually keeps this chain in stock.

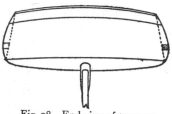

Fig. 98.   End view of transom

The transom looks very square at the sides, as it now is, and should be finished off on each side with a "quarter badge," a piece of wood 1/16 of an inch thick that carries out the face of the transom, rounding ⅛ of an inch on each side. This is protected and strengthened by a wedge-shaped block fastened to

Fig. 99.   Side view of transom

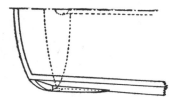

Fig. 100.   Top view of transom

the ship's side that backs up against this side piece or "quarter badge" on the stern so that anything scraping along the side would be carried out around and not meet a square corner on which to catch and rip off the wood. This "quarter badge" is all that has survived of the elaborate quarter galleries with their many windows and carved figures and floral designs that beautified the sterns of sixteenth century ships.

The transom decorations may be constructed in various ways, by using either a thin strip of brass or a piece of cord, gilded and tacked on, or the whole may be carved out of one piece of wood and set in flush. However it is done the design is the same, a gilded, rope arch over the top and another following the deck crown, the two forming a panel, with her name in gilded letters therein and below it the name of her home port, New York.

Fig. 101. Transom decorations

The stem of the "Sea Witch" was light and graceful and ornamented up under her bowsprit with a gilded dragon with outspread wings, fiery tongue, and the usual round turn in the long, tapering tail, ending in a fish-tail farther down on each side of the stem. I made a very effective little dragon by folding over a thin piece of shim brass and with small scissors cutting out the shape of the dragon shown on the plans. The top of the stem was cut away to a wedge and after spreading the two sides of the dragon apart and filling in between the two sides of the head with a drop of solder it was

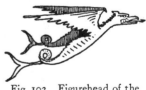

Fig. 102. Figurehead of the "Sea Witch"

tacked into place by a pin head put into the loops of the tail. The dragon was then touched up with colors to make it look as ferocious as possible. Be careful to keep the figure of the dragon so that its body runs in the same direction as the stem and parallel with it.

CHAPTER VII

The Deck Furniture

BEFORE adding anything more on the outside of the hull, that might get broken in handling, it is better practice to now put on all the deck furniture. A great deal of character can be expressed in a model if the style of architecture employed in the construction of deck fittings is correct for the period in which the ship was built.

The "Sea Witch" was built when American ships were in their prime; when the sombre green had given way to pure white painted bulwarks inside. Waterways, bulkheads and deck-houses harmonized with the decks and were kept as clean and white as a man-of-war's by holystones and prayer books. The paint was always kept spotless by soogy-moogy and hard scrubbing.

There are two kinds of finish to woodwork at sea — bright work and paint work. Bright work includes all surfaces that are kept scraped clean to the bare wood and either oiled or varnished; while paint work, of course, means surfaces that are painted.

The bright work, on such ships as the "Sea Witch," included the decks, gangway ladders, capstan bars, wheel and the round-turned portion of the stanchions to the poop rail. Some ships also kept bright the frames to the rods that fitted in the windows between the glass inside and the solid, wooden sliding shutters on the outside, while others had these narrow frames painted a bright red.

The poop rail and the square portions at the top and bottom of the poop rail stanchions, as well as the main rail and waterways, were kept painted pure white on American ships. You could spot a British ship in a second's glance by her varnished poop rails, wheel box, companionway, skylights and often the whole forward deck-house, because, being built of teak, these kept well preserved under a varnish or oil finish. But in American ships all these were painted white, giving a cleaner look along her decks than the dark spots of teak did on the other ships which gave their decks a heavier, more littered-up appearance to the eye.

The entrance to the after cabin, by means of a coach house at the forward end of the poop deck, was a characteristic American style of finish, having its overhanging roof on the forward end supported on heavy brackets resplendant in carved scrolls and vine effects and affording a shelter that permitted the window in front being kept open even in rainy weather. It projected forward of the poop just enough to permit of a doorway in either side with a high sill to keep out surface water that might be sloshing around on deck. It extended aft onto the poop, giving a long, low appearance. But for this it would have stuck up square, like a cab on an old style locomotive and been very unsightly.

Another characteristic feature of American deck finish was the many small, horizontal panels in the doors. All these are small features in themselves, yet to the eye they gave a lower appearance than the long, vertical panels which made the deck-houses on British ships appear higher and more awkward than need be. American shipbuilders strove to make their ships appear balanced and harmonious along their decks. I have seen some beautiful, foreign-built ships, their hulls symmetrical in every line and as sweet and fair in their curves as an artist could paint a ship, only to find a square, box-like, teak structure set up on deck that looked as if it did not belong to the ship at all.

Even the planks of the forward deck-house, in ships like the "Sea Witch," were run fore and aft so that by their lines they gave a longer, lower appearance than if they had been planked up vertically and all windows and shutters were about once and a half or twice their height in length.

The roofs of all houses and skylights had a generous overhang and were well filleted out with moulding beneath so they had a solid look to them and a far better balanced appearance than houses with but little ex-tension to the edge of the roof (Fig. 103).

Fig. 103

A heavy piece, like a waterway, was raised around the edges on top of all the houses (the small, sky-light tops and the cuddy or companionway tops were made flush) and fitted at the lower corners with lead scupper pipes. This prevented the rain from leaving streak marks down over the clean, white, painted sides and also made it handy to put a barrel under to catch the fresh water — often a priceless necessity at sea.

In the tropics we used to plug the main deck scuppers and collect about six inches of water in which all hands would flounder around and have a good bath and then spread out our blankets in it, soap them and wash them by treading on them. Such days of luxury were but few at sea.

The deck being only about four inches thick, while the waterways along the side of the ship were ten to twelve inches thick and composed of three pieces, twelve inches wide, quite a puddle could collect at the scuppers. When it became deep enough to flow over the top of the water-ways there were places where it could leak out.

The bulwarks fitted down fairly snug on the water-ways, but there were three or four of the squares between timber-heads where the bulwarks had been cut out and hinged sections put on, hinged at the top and lashed fast in ordinary weather, that were not altogether water-tight. When a ship got well below Rio, on her voyage around Cape Horn, and bad weather was about to be encountered these lashings were cut, allowing these "freeing ports," as they are called, to swing open when a big sea flooded the decks and so help to relieve the ship of this weight of water which the small two inch lead pipe scuppers could not begin to drain away. The main deck scuppers were flanged and nailed down flat to the ship's side planking, but the deck house scuppers stuck out a few inches so that the water dripped clear of the side of the house and would not leave a disfiguring, slobbery stain below it.

To build the "Sea Witch's" forward deck-house, take two pieces of ⅛ inch pine, ⅞ of an inch wide and 2¾ inches long for the two sides and two pieces 1⅞ inches long for the two ends.

Lay out the doors and windows on the two sides as shown in the plan. The forward end has no windows or doors and the after end a door only, leading to the galley.

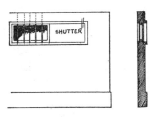

Fig. 104. Forward deck house window

The top of the windows lay off ⅛ of an inch down from the top edge and the bottom 3/16 of an inch below it. The windows are ¼ inch in length, fore and aft, and a sliding shutter should be represented aft of each window, sliding in a batten at top and bottom (Fig. 104). This batten can be chiseled so that it stands out in relief about 1/32 of an inch. The edges of the shutter can be scratched in but the grating frame in the window will have to be carved or notched down a six-teenth of an inch and then the window cut clear through. On the inside of the window cut away a ledge about 1/16 of an inch all around and about 1/16 of an inch deep and in this recess fit a piece of celluloid — an old photographic film is just the thing to imitate glass. The grating can be made of some very fine wire; pins are almost too heavy, but bank pins will do. Bore them down from the top and push them in so that they just go into the bottom frame and if you are careful to get them all plumb and parallel you will have a good resemblance to a ship's window.

The painting is the hardest part, in order to get it well coated and yet not gummed-up with too thick paint. In-stead of rubbing down with sandpaper, use a very fine file, one of the die sinker set of files, and clean out the corners square and neat, after the paint has dried and hardened.

The doors can be either cut in, showing their narrow, horizontal panels, or made of 1/16 inch wood and hinged on. Actual hinges as small as needed for these doors are an impossible item to make, but hinging a door can be accomplished by sticking the point of a bank pin into the lower part at its hinge edge and pushing the door into its recess cut in the side of the house, and then running the point of a bank pin down from the top, cutting off the pin as soon as its point enters the top edge of the door suffi-ciently to hold it. Doors so hinged will open and close, but must, of course, be very gingerly handled. The fact that they will open, showing the house to be hollow, gen-erally excites some little comment from critics who are looking the model over. When all sides of the house are ready, cut the corners to a mitre joint so that the seam is right on the corner and then fasten them with glue and bank pins the heads of which are snipped off and driven in flush.

After the glue has set well, shape the bottom so that it fits the arch or crown of the deck and cut the top edges to give a similar round before you put on the roof, which should overhang an eighth of an inch and be shaped as previously described. A couple of pins slanted down through the sides and into the deck, with the heads afterwards snipped off and driven in flush with a fine nail-punch, together with glue, will hold this house in place on deck.

Space off the location of the masts and bore holes for them through the deck — a $\frac{1}{4}$ inch hole for the mizzen mast and 5/16 inch holes for the main and foremast.

The hatchways can be cut out with a penknife. Don't finish them until you have made and put on the hatch coamings. Take $\frac{1}{8}$ inch thick wood, $\frac{1}{4}$ inch wide, and cut out a notch 1/16 of an inch square along one edge. You will need about twenty inches of this to frame the three hatchways. It doesn't matter how the corners are joined, for after all is painted you cannot see how it is put together. But they must show a ledge, all around inside where you notched them down, forming a recess to take the hatch covers.

Hatchways on real ships were generally built up in two pieces, the lower one often worked out with a cove or hollow, although some builders did not use this little refinement but carried them up vertically.

The main and after hatch being so large there was generally a fore-and-aft centerpiece called the "strong-

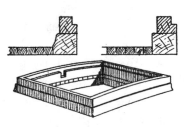

Fig. 105. Hatchway

back," that fitted into a notch at the forward and after ends of the inside of the hatch coaming, and that had a rabbet worked along each of the upper edges so that the recess for the hatch cover was continuous around each side. The covers were of material as heavy as the deck plank and had short, beam reinforcements underneath, so they were quite heavy. They were made into small sections, so that two men, one at each opposite corner, could take hold of the ring-bolts there and lift them off. These ring-bolts were fitted to drop flush into circular grooves so that they would not chafe through the tarpaulin hatch-covers when the hatches were battened down for sea. A hatch on a ship like the "Sea Witch" would have three sections on each side.

When all her cargo was in, the seams around these hatches were well-caulked with oakum and then "payed," or poured full of hot pitch, to seal them up perfectly water-tight. Over this was then laid two and sometimes three tarpaulins—water-tight canvas—which were battened down or held securely by flat, iron strips fitting over staples driven into the hatch coaming, the battens having slots to match the staples; and these were squeezed tight against the coamings by means of pegs of wood driven into the staples, so that they acted as wedges against the battens (Fig. 106). Besides these battens, around all four sides there were one or two iron battens, of about one-half inch by two inch iron, that hooked into other staples at the forward end of the hatch and jammed down over two vertical staples at the after end and were pegged fast (Fig. 107).

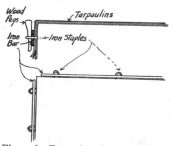

Fig. 106. Fastenings for hatch-covers

These were to prevent the tarpaulins from bulging in a gale of wind and being torn off by the seas that sometimes broke, solid water, onto the decks and hatches.

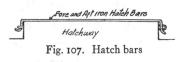

Fig. 107. Hatch bars

In speaking of hatchways we said it did not matter how the corners were joined and one may therefore be tempted into making them the easiest way, that is, with simply a mitre joint — each piece cut at an angle of 45 degrees. But you will find when you try to squeeze these corners together in glue that it is very difficult to get a true, square hatchway, as they will slide about out of square very easily. I prefer to make a mortise, and tenon-cut or halve one down on top of the other, working them into shape in pairs, two sides and two ends, so that when you finish them with a file you know both are exactly the same length. When you put these ends together with glue and squeeze them up tight, there is a square end to butt instead of a bevel to ride and slip about most exasperatingly.

A real ship's hatchway is put together with dove-tailed mortise and tenon ends, the most solid construction that can be made, but when you consider the strain put upon it by caulking, it is none too strong. The forward hatch is a smaller one, but the after hatch is about the same size as the main hatch.

There has to be some way of getting below, into the ship, for all the provisions, barrels of beef, pork, flour and bread are stowed away aft in the stern where, owing to the sharp shape of the ship, cargo stowage is difficult. A large iron tank, in which the most of the ship's fresh water is carried, is built to fit in aft under the cabin floor and there is also a place to stow the extra sails, with which all ships are provided, for a voyage made without blow-

ing some sails to ribbons is unusual. Most ships have a
new and an old suit of sails. The old suit is worn while
the ship is rolling and slapping her sails against the
masts, in "flying-fish weather," around the equator. But
as she gets far south or north, where strong winds are encountered, all of these old, patched sails are unbent, one
by one, and the newer, stronger sails are substituted, to
be replaced again with the older canvas after the ship has
rounded the "Horn."

To give access below to these various necessities, a
"booby hatch," as the raised, box-like structure over the
after hatch is called, is lashed down at each corner to
ring-bolts fastened in the deck. This is high enough off
the deck (the hatch coamings only being about one foot)
to keep out the seas that may break aboard and slosh half
a foot deep across the deck. A sliding companionway is
fitted on top of the booby hatch and by removing one section of the hatch covers below, access can be had to the
sail locker, ship's stores, etc. The fresh water tank has
a pipe leading up to a deck plate so that water can be obtained without going below, by unscrewing this deck
plate and screwing in a small pump by which to raise the
water into buckets.

The corners of this booby hatch were usually rounded
a little, as were nearly all corners on deck fittings, for the
seas have a way of coming aboard and playing at nine-
pins, with the men for the pins, and when you are knocked
off your feet and go skidding across the deck, sharp corners are dangerous. Ribs enough were broken, even
against rounded corners.

Some ships had hard pine corner posts that made a
smart looking finish when kept scraped bright and varnished; but it only made so much more "ginger bread"

work for the sailors to scrape and keep in order and many captains did not like their appearance.

Between the mizzenmast and the steering wheel is a small, square, flat-topped skylight and a companionway leading to the main saloon and captain's quarters aft. The mates' rooms were generally in the forward end of the poop deck and these officers used the coach house doors to reach the deck.

Up to the year 1800, and in some cases for several years later, ships generally had long, wooden tillers that swung across under the deck beams supported on a wooden, athwartship beam, just below the deck beams and the steering wheels were farther forward than as shown on the "Sea Witch." They were just abaft the mizzenmast. But the use of iron tillers, much shorter and often fitted abaft the rudder head, moved the steering wheel away aft. The tiller ropes were rove off below decks, though many ships, as late as 1880, had them rove off above the deck, with just a shallow box, like a hood, to keep the turn of the steering drum or barrel, as it was variously termed, dry and protected.

On the "Sea Witch," the tackle was below decks, coming up over sheaves vertically to the steering wheel drum and covered with a box to keep it dry, the top of the box being removable to give access to the ropes and drum.

Wooden steering wheels were almost universally used on ships of any size until about the time of the "Sea Witch," that is, along in the 1840's; but about that time American shipbuilders introduced many innovations aboard their ships that soon excited the admiration and envy of all other nations. Patented pumps, windlasses, iron capstans, geared-up hand winches, iron steering wheels and many new bits of iron work aloft that simplified the ship's gear, were introduced and a few years later, in the 1850's, the Government made red and green sailing lights a compulsory part of the ship's outfit. This showed another ship how she was heading, which the white light on the bowsprit cap, previously carried, did not do.

These lights had boards, to which they were fastened by hooks and lashings, to act as screens so that the lights could not show across the ship and cause confusion, but only ahead. These light-boards were lashed up a short distance on the fore-shrouds, but as they were sometimes hidden by the foot of the foresail, some ships had them fastened to light iron davits, aft on the quarters, that were swung out at night. These had the advantage of being where the officer of the deck could see that they were lighted and they also were well out so that they were visible past the sails and more protected. Later ships, especially large, foreign-built vessels, had two small lighthouses, as they were termed, built one on either side of the after end of the forecastle head in which the side-lights were placed.

The steering wheels were four to five feet in diameter, the lower spokes just clearing the deck. On wooden wheels, the uppermost spoke, when the rudder was directly amidships, was usually turned so that it had several ridges that could be felt on a dark night so that the man steering the ship could tell by the feel of it how the rudder was located. This spoke was termed the "king-spoke." On iron steering wheels, a small, fancy-rope grommet was generally fitted so that it could be recognized in the same way.

The wheel stood away from the wheel-box far enough to permit a man to stand behind the wheel and to prevent the chafe of the man's boots on the deck, a hardwood grating was always laid out on the deck on each side of the wheel, for the helmsman must always stand on the weather or windward side of his wheel.

Besides the reserve supply of fresh water down in the run, as the lower, after-part of the ship is called, there were two large coopered casks held against the after-part of the forecastle, on each side, by four iron straps that went through the deck and side of the forecastle, strapping them down solidly into the saddles fitted to the deck and into which they set. These were about six feet long, four feet high, and two and a half or two feet wide, with rounded corners. The staves of these casks were about two inch oak and the heads were set in at the ends an inch or so.

The water in these casks was used up first. Every morning the bung was removed and the ship's cook pumped out his day's allowance and a quart per man per day was doled out to the crew. In our ship we had nothing but a wooden deck bucket to hold this water, which was stowed in a spare bunk in the forecastle. In hot weather this bucket was bone-dry by noontime and not another drop could we get until the next day. We drank rain water when we could get it fresh enough to be palatable, but desperation drove us to making "bung dippers," small, long, canvas bags that would go down through the bung-hole, and though the mates saw to it personally that the bung was driven in hard with a hammer or mallet, before sundown each day, we used to take turns in straining at that bung until we removed it and stole water enough to satisfy our craving for a drink.

Around each mast on deck there are bitts and rails on which to belay the gear that handles the spars and sails up aloft. These consist of two, stout, vertical pieces, eight to ten inches square in a real ship, with a bolster or cross-piece, about six inches by ten inches, across their forward side, to which the topsail sheets make fast. Extending aft, on each side, is the belaying pin rail, about three inches by six inches in size. At the foremast these butt against the forecastle house. The main, carry aft of the mainmast far enough to mount the flywheels of the pumps on and are supported, mid-length and at the after-end, by a stanchion to the deck. The mizzen, go aft of the mast and have stanchions at the end only, they being so short.

In making these, notch the forward side of the bitts and the after side of the bolster so that the latter crosses the bitts about ⅛ of an inch from the top of the bitts (Fig. 108). Glue and squeeze them tightly together. The forward edge of the bolster should extend beyond the bitts about 1/16 of an inch

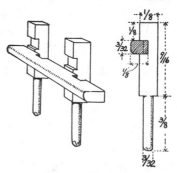

when in place. Chamfer the corners of the top of the bitt and the forward side of the bolster should also be well rounded on its edges. This is necessary to prevent chafing and cutting of the topsail sheets which carry a heavy strain and are belayed by a round-turn around this bolster piece.

Fig. 108. Fitting the bolster to the bitts

The bitts stand 9/16 of an inch above the deck, on the model. Below that, round them off, peg-shaped, to drive with glue into holes bored in the deck just forward of the masts. The side pin-rails should have their forward ends notched down and rounded into peg-ends to fit into holes drilled into the after-side of the bitts, about level with the bolster and fastened to the deck by bank pins put down through the middle of each stanchion. The stan-

Fig. 109.
Stanchion

chions should all be turned down spindle-shaped.

Small, brass, belaying pins 5/16 of an inch in length can be purchased from dealers in ship model supplies. You can snip these off to ¼ of an inch in length and drill holes every 3/32 of an inch apart, putting a pin in each hole. In the pin rail, along the side of the ship from the poop to forecastle head, you will need some, not so close of course, only opposite each mast, under the shrouds, where about a dozen are required, and a couple opposite the forward end of the main hatch, for the fore lower yard and topsail yard braces. Four are needed on each side in the after-end of the forecastle head deck, out near the sides, for the jib sheets to belay to.

Pumps of all kinds, from time to time, have been used on ships, varying with the size of the ship, from home-made, square, wooden box pumps to the endless-chain pumps that threw such a quantity of water that they were the favorite pump on men-of-war. There they had room to rig up such pumps, and with long, extended cranks, gangs of men could get hold to turn the sprocket wheel over which the chain ran with its continuous succession of washer-like valves. On smaller vessels, using plunger pumps, the crank arm was hinged in the center and operated alternately, a plunger on each side. A cross arm, on the end of the crank arm, enabled four or five men to lay hold of it on each side of the ship. Modern wind-lasses, that operate by this method, are today known as pump-brake windlasses.

The flywheel plunger or diaphragm pump used on the "Sea Witch" was an innovation and to make it is a nice and very particular little job. Get a ring the right diameter or bend one out of brass wire to a ⅝ inch diameter and solder the ends together. Then bend two S-shaped spokes, flattening them where they cross, to make them lay snug, and solder them together and to the rim (Fig. 110). Bend the crank out of one piece of wire, from side to side, and here is where the difficulty comes in, for in trying to solder this fast, snug up to the corner where the spokes cross at the hub, you are likely to unsolder all you already have stuck together. Don't use a straight-spoked gear-wheel out of some clock or watch. It cheapens the whole model.

Flatten the ends of the wires that make the plungers and it looks much better when bent around the crank than if the wire is left round. The pump wells can be made of two pieces of a very small diameter brass or copper tubing, left standing about 1/16 of an inch above the deck.

Where the pump-crank rests on the pin rail, bend a thin piece of brass or tin (the top of a condensed milk can), cut into a strip 1/16 of an inch wide and fasten it with the head end of a bank pin cut so that it just goes through the pin rail.

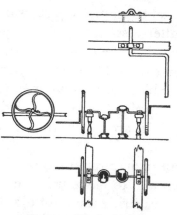

Fig. 110. Flywheel pump

Paint the handles, spokes and cranks black, but the rim of the wheel should be a bright red — a vermillion color.

The various ways ships carried their life boats are as numerous as the different types of ships. The larger the ship the more boats she had to carry for the number of people she had aboard. So we find old merchant ships of about 1800, with one long boat stowed on deck, amidships, while a ship-of-war of the same period would carry about six or eight, and large ships of the line, three-deckers, carried as many as twelve boats. A frigate carried nine boats, sloops-of-war six boats, and brigs five boats.

Merchant ships have much smaller crews than men-of-war and the shipping rules formulated by the insurance companies regulated the number of boats they should carry, based on a rule that allowed ten cubic feet of boat space, below the gunwale, per man.

So we find clippers such as "Sea Witch," with two long boats stowed, bottom up on skids, on top of the forecastle and a pair of quarter-boats, a lighter type of boat, generally a whale boat or sharp-built cutter, hung on davits where they could be quickly got afloat in case of emergency.

Some idea of the size of the boats carried by men-of-war can be ascertained by the following rule in vogue when ships-of-war were sailing craft, unspoiled by the introduction of machinery. For the length of the first launch, multiply the square root of the ship's length by 2.6. The boat's beam was one-fourth of her length. The first and second cutters, for ships-of-the-line, and the second cutters, for sloops-of-war, were to be 9/10 the length of the launch. The third and fourth cutters, for ships-of-the-line, and the second cutters, for sloops-of-war, were to be 9/10 the length of the first cutter. Quarter, waist or stern boats were to be the same dimension as the second cutter for sloops-of-war, but to be built lighter. Gigs were the same length as the latter.

Two twenty-four foot long-boats, stowed bottom up on skids, with a galley smoke-stack, of the Liverpool type or revolving top that always turned so that the smoke-opening was to leeward, and a hatch over the galley and forecastle, will finish off this part of the model.

Paint the galley smoke-stack black and all the rest white, although some ships had the tops of all their houses and hatches painted a very faint tint of yellow, orange or blue. The skid-beams were cut out on their lower edge, so they only touched the top of the house in the center and on each side, leaving a clear drainage below and room to pass lashings over the long-boats to hold them down on the skids (Fig. 111). This is very necessary, for many a boat has been smashed into kindling wood by a sea breaking aboard, and if left unlashed might do no end of damage by being washed around the deck, like a battering ram, to smash things.

Away aft, alongside the wheel-box, should be fitted a small eighteen inch square hatch, the entrance to which is called the "lazarette," a sort of spare, gear-storage

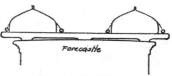

Fig. 111. Skid-beams

space which gives access to the tiller and wheel ropes of the ship. Sometimes there is a hatch on each side of the ship, but generally one is all that is provided, and that on the starboard side.

Deck ladders giving easy access to the raised, poop deck aft and the forecastle head forward, are delicate things to make for a model, being only about 1¼ inches thick on the real ship and made of hard wood and varnished, so they cannot be made too thin for the model.

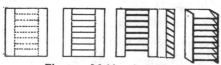

Fig. 112. Making the ladder

One very good way is to make them of brass or copper and solder in the treads or steps. Another way is to lay the ladder out, expanded on a sheet of thin copper. Cut out each step with a sharp, small chisel, leaving a very

little spot, uncut, at the back of each step and then bend
or fold over the two sides (Fig. 112).

If you warm the copper a little it is less liable to break
the tiny, uncut spot which holds the steps in position until you can tip them underneath with solder to hold them
securely. Such a ladder is very strong, when done, and
the side-pieces can be cut to the angle required. I find
it a good plan to shape the top edge, but leave the lower
ends of these side-pieces square; then crease the deck
with a knife point and push these square corners down
into the deck and your ladders are held securely in position with no other fastenings to bother with.

Straight ladders will do, but if you want an extra fine
finish, as most clippers were fitted off, make these ladders so that the side rails have a slight double-curve to

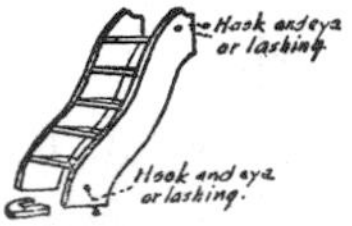

Fig. 113. Curved-
rail ladder

them, as shown in sketch herewith (Fig.
113). To ascend these steep steps, for
they were steep, there was a small, oak
stanchion set vertically each side of them
going from the deck up through a socket
on the edge of the higher deck and extending up about thirty inches above that deck. Through
the top of these hand-rope stanchions, a pair of fancy
cotton hand-ropes were rove with turk's heads in their
upper ends, pointed and worked to a grommet on their
lower ends, which was seized fast to the lower part of the
ladders so that a person could grasp these two ropes and
steady himself against the heave of the ship and at the
same time pull himself up the ladder.

The ladders to the poop were fitted one on each side,
well out to the side of the ship, but not so far that their
lower ends were up on waterways. Forward there was
one ladder to the forecastle head (some call this the top-
gallant-forecastle, but at sea it is shortened to "fo'csl

head") amidships, where there was room clear of the fore hatch, as on the "Sea Witch." Where there was not room, there were ladders on each side. Under the center of the after-end of the forecastle head there was always a turned stanchion supporting the after beam of that deck.

The older style of windlass, not going as far back as the real old ones used in the 17th century, where wooden handspikes or heavers were used to turn the horizontal log windlass which had holes staggered at intervals around it into which the heavers could be inserted and readily removed, was what is known as the pump-break windlass. Ratchets, operating on a large-diameter toothed or gear wheel, on each side of the windlass, were connected by vertical rods to levers extending athwartships, on each side of the forecastle head, that were pivoted on the heavy sampson post, amidship, and fitted with wooden handles at right angles to the levers, so that about four men could lay hold of them on each side of the deck. More men used to lay hold by standing inside the handle, for when the anchor was apeak and it came to breaking it loose from the bottom into which it was well embedded, if the bottom happened to be a sticky kind of clay, all hands were sometimes insufficient to break the anchor's hold and in that case sail had to be set and the ship, by her weight propelled by the wind, used to free the anchor.

A far more powerful windlass was the kind that had a bevel gear fitted and a small gear engaged into it at the bottom of the vertical spindle of a capstan, up on the forecastle head. With capstan bars a man could exercise more power by pushing than he could by pulling up and down where only his weight counted and muscles could not be brought into play as they could on a capstan bar.

These single capstans were soon supplanted by what were called "double-acting capstans," fitted with two sets of capstan-bar holes. The lower gave simply a straight push on the gear below. By shipping the bars into the separate set of holes above these and going around the capstan the opposite way, a multiplicity of gears turned the windlass only half as fast, but they doubled its power and few were the times when the anchor failed to break out when the "double-action" was resorted to.

The "Sea Witch" was fitted with a double-acting capstan which had the rounded head peculiar to this type

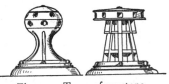

Fig. 114. Types of capstans

and not the square run where the bars were shipped in, which was popular on older types of ships, particularly men-of-war.

Racks to hold the capstan bars were fitted so that the bars lay horizontally, inside the rail around the forecastle head, two-deep, just forward of the cat-heads. The rest stood up vertically in

Fig. 115. Capstan bar rack

racks fitted on the after-side of the foremast or against the forward side of the house, between the pin rails or fife rails as they are variously termed. Capstan bars were always kept scraped bright and varnished or oiled. By "bright," a word we have often used, is meant being scraped down to bare wood. "Bright decks" mean unpainted, bare boards; and "bright spars" means the same, unpainted, showing the natural color of the wood.

Sticking out beyond the bluff of the bows, on either side, is a timber a foot square, called the "cat-heads." The function of these is to form a derrick by which the anchors may be hoisted up clear of the water. In their outboard ends, three vertical slots are cut and sheaves are inserted, just as if it were a triple-block, over which a stout rope, called the "cat-fall," is rove through a treble-block below, which has a large, very strong hook on its lower end, which hooks into the ring of the anchor when it is about to be hoisted up. The inboard end of this "cat-fall," or tackle, which is all it is, leaving off the nautical phraseology, is taken around the capstan and so the anchor is hoisted.

The inboard end of the "cat-head" is butted against a vertical post of the same size. This seemingly excess-strength is needed, for when a ship goes to sea her anchors are hoisted up and the flukes or hook-like ends are swung inboard and lashed with small chains to these timbers; and as these anchors weigh three or four tons each, the necessity for excessive strength about everything pertaining to the ground tackle, as the anchors and cables are termed, can be appreciated.

In order to raise the anchors up on the bows of the ship, after they have been "catted," or hoisted up as far as the blocks under the "cat-head" will permit, a heavy piece of cable is passed around the topmast-head and stopped fast with old canvas, laid and wrapped under it to prevent chafing the other rigging. This hangs down about even with the foremast-head where a large, three-sheave block is hooked in with a double-block well below it, forming a tackle, the running-end coming down through a snatch-block hooked into an eyebolt or ring-bolt in the deck, just aft of the "cat-head," and from there it goes to the capstan. This double-block hooks into a chain, the lower end of which has a large iron hook that is lowered down and swung until the hook catches around the fluke of the anchor. It is fishing with a pretty good-sized hook. When securely hooked, this chain is hooked, as before stated, to the double-block and the crew wind the fall around the capstan and so lift the anchor up onto the bows.

As the strain of this tackle is inboard, the anchor, when it reaches the rail, scrapes the side of the ship about its own length aft of the "cat-head," and just at that place the side of the ship is protected by being padded out flush with the rails and sheathed with iron.

A cup-like casting is fitted right on top of this so that the fluke of the anchor can be hooked into it and the anchor left there temporarily in case there is likelihood that it might be needed again soon. Small chain lashings are usually passed around it here and made fast to a ring-bolt in the deck.

If being stowed for a long voyage, the flukes are raised with the fish-tackle, clear above the rail, another tackle being hooked on so that it can pull forward, as the anchor will have a strong inclination to swing aft and inboard. The anchor is then lowered to the deck and with capstan bars, as heavers, it is shoved up close to and lashed around the post at the heel of the "cat-head."

All this fish-tackle fall is taken down and stowed away when the ship's anchors are stowed; but ships in port generally have it in place which probably accounts for its being shown on so many models. But it is an ungainly affair and spoils the clean, ship-shape appearance of a ship model.

When the anchors are stowed on the bows, with their great, wooden stocks standing up vertical and lashed fast aft of the "cat-heads," the cables are unshackled, pulled inboard through the hawse pipes and the latter are stopped with a plug, pulled in tight and held fast by a lashing inside under the forecastle head.

On top of the "cat-head," between the rail and the post inboard, put in four small eyes made of bent bank pins,

and into the deck, just forward of the "cat-head," four
more. The various jib sheets make fast to the latter eyes
and the hauling ends reeve through those on top of the
"cat-heads," which are lignum-vitæ bulls-eyes in the real
ship, stapled down to the "cat-head," and lead aft to belaying pins on the edge of the forecastle head deck.

Hᴇᴇʟ-Tᴀᴘᴘᴇʀ Fɪsʜɪɴɢ Sᴄʜᴏᴏɴᴇʀ

CHAPTER VIII

THE ANCHORS

BEFORE we finish off our model with chain-plates, channels and a monkey rail around the poop aft, let us consider the question of anchors.

In the 17th century, when hemp cables were generally in use, the rule for proportioning the size of these cables was to make their circumference one-half inch for every foot of beam the ship was wide; and the weight of one hundred and twenty fathoms of cable was found to be one-fifth the square of their circumference. A twenty-four inch cable therefore was found, by multiplying twenty-four by twenty-four and dividing the product by five, to weigh 115 1/5 pounds per fathom and one hundred and twenty fathoms therefore would weigh 13,824 pounds. This was the master cable or the heaviest one in the ship and according to the rule then in vogue, the anchor should weigh one-half the weight of its cable, which would be 6,912 pounds for the heaviest anchor for a ship forty-eight feet in beam, or that of a first-rate, as ships were then classed. The large ships carried eight anchors and the small, five or six.

The shape of anchors has often been changed and many different kinds have been patented, but the old anchors in use in the days of which we are speaking of were all made to a certain rule. The two arms with their flukes or palms, formed the arc of a circle whose center was ⅜ of the shank from the end the flukes were fastened to; and each arm was ⅜ of the shank in length. The flukes or palms were just half the length of the arms, and their breadth across the widest part was two-fifths of the

85

length of the arms. In thickness, the shank, at the throat or juncture with the arms, was in circumference 1/5 its length and at the small end 2/3 of that at the throat end.

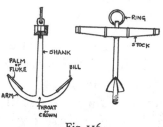

Fig. 116

The small end of the arms of the flukes was ¾ of the circumference of the shank at the throat.

To find the weight of an anchor in pounds, divide the cube of the length of the stock in inches by 1160. By applying this rule to our model, an anchor 1½ inches long, equal to twelve feet, would give an anchor of 2,574 pounds, which is just about the weight of an anchor for such a ship and by this rule the other dimensions of the anchor can be ascertained.

The anchor-stock looks like a huge balk of wood, on a real anchor, yet, like masts, they are not all in one piece. Anchor-stocks are made in two halves, mortises cut in each and clamped fast about the stock, which has a slight shoulder at this point. Four square bands of flat iron were driven on, like hoops on a barrel, as the stock tapers, until they clamped the wood solid against the shank. They should not come together, wood and wood, but always have a slight opening to permit squeezing up as the stock shrinks. The stock is about 2½ times the size of the shank, in the middle, and its length is equal to that of the shank. The top edge is left straight across, but the bottom and sides taper so that the ends are one-half the size the stock is in the middle. The hoops or bands are driven on, two near the middle and one near each end of the stock.

Hemp cables had been superseded by chain about 1813, or long before the "Sea Witch" was built. A chain suitable for her weight of anchors would, on the real ship, be made of iron 1⅝ inches in diameter, so get small lavelier chain, as in the case of the rudder chains. Don't use too heavy a chain. It should really be a stud-link chain (Fig.

Fig. 117. Studding chain

117), one with a brace or stud to keep the link from flattening down when a heavy strain is put upon it; but this you will have to forego, unless the model is built on a scale larger than ⅛ inch. The chain cable should shackle to the ring of the anchor and its end be fastened into the hawse-hole in the ship's bow just below the main deck and about ⅜ of

Fig. 118. Shackle

an inch out from the middle of the ship on each side. Paint the inside of the hawse-hole vermillion. Bore this hole in only about a quarter of an inch or even less. Bend the end of a bank pin into an eye hooked into the anchor chain end and stick the pin up into this hole until it is out of sight. Don't let the chain loop down too loosely. Have it fairly snug, but not drawn tightly, either, up to the "cat-head" and the anchor.

To make an anchor seems difficult, but after one or two have been turned out you will find it an easy job. To make an anchor for the "Sea Witch" you will need one piece of ⅛ inch square brass or copper, for the stock (I use a copper wire nail and file it square), 1½ inches long, and another piece for the arms, 1 5/16 inches long and of the same size. File the shank-piece so it tapers slightly, only about 1/32 of an inch, being reduced at the ring end. Bend the arm piece so that it makes a right-angle bend. Then file the heavy end of the shank down to about 1/32 of an inch in diameter for a distance of ⅛ of an inch. Drill a hole through the arm, right at the bend, and put the shank end through this hole and rivet it there (Fig.

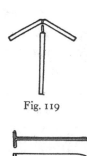

Fig. 119

Fig. 120. Paper
fastener

119). You can solder it of course, without all this trouble, but in heating the arms, to solder on the flukes, the shank is apt to drop off. I have tried that; also beveling one down on to the other; but find the method described far safer and quicker in the long run. The flukes can be cut out of any thin brass or copper. I found some large, paper fasteners (Fig. 120) came in just right for this and they were of thin brass which was easily cut off to shape desired.

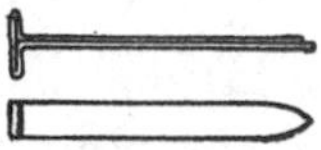

The soldering outfit necessary for this light work is simplicity itself. An empty, drawing-ink bottle, only about 1½ inches in diameter and an inch or so high, with a piece of brass tubing set through the cork so that it stands up about an inch, makes a splendid lamp with a round-corded wick fitted through the tube down into the wood alcohol with which the bottle is then filled (Fig.

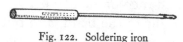

Fig. 121. Lamp
for soldering

121). For a soldering iron, take a piece of about ⅛ inch copper wire, four inches long, and stick one end into a piece of pine shaped into a round handle. File the end of the wire tapered to a point and as soon as you buy a small box of soldering paste or get half a cup full of soldering fluid from a plumber and buy from him a stick of half-and-half solder, you are fitted out to do all the soldering you will need on a model ship.

The anchor is the heaviest piece of metal you have to solder. To handle the parts you will need a pointed pair of pliers and a pair of tweezers. Heat the ends of the arms of the anchor and touch the top edge, where you want the flukes to stick, with the

Fig. 122. Soldering iron

soldering paste or fluid. Treat the flukes the same. This cleans the metal of all grease and dirt and makes the solder stick.

I have not had much success with this so-called string solder. It acts too much like lead and rolls up into balls and can't be persuaded to stick. But if you take half-and-half stick solder and melt it in a pan, over the stove, and then take it out on the sidewalk and pour a long, thin trail of it on the stones, you can use these thin strips to better advantage. It will melt quicker in the small flame you use. Save every little bubble of it for you only use an infinitesimal amount at any one time.

Heat the flukes of the anchor and touch a drop of solder on each. Then turn this over against the arm of your anchor and holding it in place with a pair of pincers put it into the flame a few seconds and it will be stuck fast. You must hold it securely for several seconds after you remove it from the flame to give the solder time to cool off and harden. If you don't do so it will slip out of position while the solder is yet soft. If you use too much solder you will stick your pliers fast with the squeezed-out, surplus solder. Use only a very little. That is all that is needed.

Where you rivet the shank into the arms of the anchor, you should put solder over it all. Here is where your small soldering iron comes in. Holding all in the flame, rub the lumps of solder out and spread it with the soldering iron, as needed, to fillet out the joints. Don't try to finish it off perfectly, the principal thing is to get enough solder on to fill all holes. With your small, rat-tail files and flat files you can soon shape all the lumps down to a perfect looking anchor. When the arms are securely soldered into place and both flukes set on true, take a flat file and shape down the back of the arms over the flukes

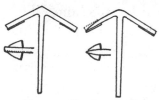

Fig. 123.   Shaping the bill
of the anchor

to a point at the nib, or bill, as the point of the fluke is called (Fig. 123).

Then bore a 1/32 of an inch hole through the end of the shank, at right angles to the arms, and bend a piece of small wire through this hole into a ring 5/16 inches in diameter, and put a touch of solder over the joint so that the anchor chain will not keep slipping out once it is shackled into it.

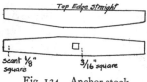

Fig. 124.   Anchor stock

The anchor stock should be the same length as the shank — 1½ inches long, 3/16 inches square for about a quarter of an inch in the middle and tapered on the bottom and sides to a scant ⅛ of an inch square on the ends (Fig. 124).

This, on such a small model, can be made of one piece with a hole bored for the shank and the stock pushed down a snug fit just below the ring. The bands can be painted on or made of very thin, shim brass soldered and driven on snug. Give the stock a coat of raw umber and the anchor itself paint a dull black. Don't use glossy, shiny paints on a model. It makes them look like toys.

CHAPTER IX

BITT-HEADS, CHANNELS, DEADEYES, ETC.

THE anchors provide for holding the ship to the ground in shallow water, but what are we going to tie her up by when she goes in alongside of a dock? She needs bow-lines, stern-lines and breast-lines. For these, regular mooring posts, called bitt-heads, are fitted on deck with holes through the bulwarks on the main deck and iron chocks fitted on top of the rail on the forecastle head and poop deck.

Use an ⅛ inch square strip of hard wood — ash, maple or oak. Allow the bitt-heads to stand 3/16 of an inch above the deck with their lower ends peg-shaped and driven with glue into holes bored into the deck 5/16 of

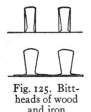

Fig. 125. Bitt-heads of wood and iron

an inch between centers. Chamfer the corners of these bitts (Fig. 125), taking more off near the deck than at the top where very little is rounded because mooring lines seldom reeve around the bitts that high and the slight downward bevel helps to keep a line from riding up and off over the top of the bitt, as the line is being slacked off. A slight surge on the line or slacking of it, will cause the rope to drop down to where the bitts are smaller and well-rounded. Put one pair of bitts on each side on the poop about ¾ of an inch from the stern and ¼ of an inch in from the side of the ship. Forward, on the main deck, abreast the fore hatchway, fit another pair about ⅛ of an inch inside of the waterways. About an inch forward of these bitts bore a hole through the solid piece of the forecastle head that forms the rail there, for the mooring line to lead out through.   About a 1/16 inch hole is big enough, about half way up between the deck and the main rail.

Just forward of the main hatch, on each side, block in solid the space between two stanchions or timber-heads and fit in a cavil, a horizontal piece of wood a scant ⅛ of an inch wide by 1/16 of an inch thick and long enough to stick forward and aft past the timber-heads ⅛ of an inch (Fig. 126), so that a mooring line can be twisted

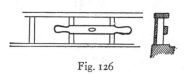

Fig. 126

around these ends, which should be chamfered on the edges so as not to cut the rope so belayed.

To hold the mooring lines at bow and stern, iron chocks are fitted; two forward on each side of the rail, on the forecastle head, and two aft on the quarter, one leading aft and one out over the side rail.   To prevent fouling the jib sheets forward, the chocks there are generally let flush into the rail (Fig. 127) and when at sea, small blocks of wood are fitted to

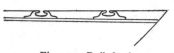

Fig. 127. Rail chocks

fill the throat of these chocks full so that no ropes can drop into them and catch, thereby causing trouble in working the ship's head-sails.

Into each side of the ship, ¾ of an inch forward of the stern and just below the rail, bore a hole and drive in with glue a scant ⅛ inch square piece of hard wood so that it sticks out 7/16 of an inch, for the main brace bumpkin. Bore a hole both vertically and horizontally near the outer end and bend an eye on each end of each of these wires (Fig. 128).   To the after one and the lower one fit very small chain (22 links to the inch, as on the rudder) and fasten one aft at the transom and the other directly below the bumpkin into the main deck waterways.   These

act as braces to counteract the pull put upon the end of
the bumpkin by the main brace, the pennant of which is
hooked into the forward eye, and also the pull up caused
by the spanker vang which hooks into the upper one.
Put a second eye, a little inside the first, on the forward
side of the bumpkin for the standing end of the main-
topsail brace.

To hold all the ropes that support the masts so that
they will be free and out from the rail of the ship, there
are wide, shelf-like boards fitted against the side of the
ship, opposite each mast, that are called channels. These
for our ship are 2½ inches long, ¼ of an inch
wide and ⅛ of an inch thick against the side
of the ship, tapered to 1/16 of an inch in
thickness on the outer edge with the fore and
after ends slightly rounded on the outer corners and made of some such wood as mahogany that will hold fastenings well and yet
not be liable to break, as would a softer wood, such as
pine.

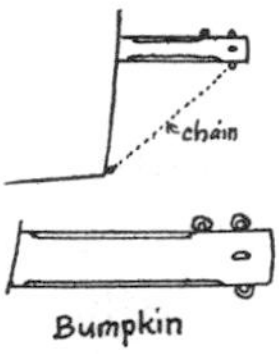

Fig. 128.
Bumpkins

The strain on the channels is so great that they would
crush in the light top-rail high above the deck which sup-
ports it. The stout timber-heads, that carry up to the
main rail below it, will carry this strain and that is where
the channels are fitted on most ships that have high rails
or, as sailors say, are deep waisted.

When the clippers began to be built larger, about 1840-
1850, and their length grew up to and beyond two hundred feet, their tonnage and weight increased so that it
was found necessary to use double channels. The upper
one as before, but below it, down against the waterways
or timbers of the ship, just below the waterways, another
channel was fitted to bring the heavy, crushing strain of

the chain-plates against something more substantial than the bulwark timbers.

These channels have to be well fastened to hold them while all the chain-plates, that take the deadeyes of the rigging in their upper ends, are being put into place. When they are on and secured they hold the channels firmly.

If you have made your model with thin, built-up bulwarks, then fasten the channels just below the main rail on the outside of the bulwarks, their forward ends even across the ship with the forward side of their respective masts, using glue and a shortened and pointed bank pin, putting it from inside through the bulwarks into the channel.

The after or mizzen channels are only 2¼ inches long, but otherwise the same as the fore and main channels.

The "Sea Witch" had six shrouds on her fore and main lower masts and four shrouds on the mizzen. So that gives us the number of deadeyes needed. Then there are two topmast-back-stays, the shrouds for that mast and those above it being close in from the tops and cross-trees up on which the ladders are made, so the men can climb aloft; one topgallant back-stay; and one each to the royal and skysail masts. The last two have no dead-eyes, but set up to bullseyes on top of the rail, so we have to provide deadeyes for six lower shrouds, two topmast and one topgallant back-stay, on each side of the fore and main masts. The mizzenmast has deadeyes for only four lower shrouds, one topmast and one topgallant back-stay on each side.

Model builders will find that data on this particular part of a ship is very difficult to find and nearly all of what is recorded is for men-of-war and not for merchant ships. For that reason a recent publication: "The Art of Rigging," by Capt. George Biddlecombe, while it looks very much the same as some other books that have been published, will be found most valuable.   It gives for merchant ships what other available books do not give. For instance, by this book, a ship rigged with hemp, as all were before the advent of the patent wire rope, which came into use in the middle of the eighteenth century, of the tonnage of the "Sea Witch," required seven shrouds, per side, on her main mast.   But the "Sea Witch" was a much easier ship on her rigging, due to the easy, fine lines of her hull, than the type of ship these rules were calculated for, and in her case six was permissible.

These deadeyes were fourteen inches in diameter, her shrouds being three inches in diameter and the lanyards which laced the upper and lower deadeyes together were 1½ inches in diameter.   The book, of course, gives all ropes' sizes by their circumferences, as was the custom then, but as the diameter is 1/3 the circumference a slight mental calculation only is needed to transpose this to the diameter size.

Space the lower deadeyes 5/16 of an inch apart, the first one forward being back about ⅛ of an inch from the end, and drill holes for the chain-plates to go through about 1/16 of an inch in from the edge.

A much easier way is to make the channels 1/16 of an inch narrower and just file notches for the chain-plates to set in, putting on a 1/16 inch strip outside, after all are in place.   By this method the copper wire which is twisted around the deadeye can be cut to length, a small eye turned in its lower end and you can then try it in place and see if it is just the right length, while the other way you have to reeve the wire through the hole in the channel and then bend in the lower eye working your pliers close up against the hull, which is not nearly so convenient.

A fourteen inch deadeye, on the scale of our model, ⅛ inch to the foot, would be about 5/32 of an inch in diameter.

If you have a small, accurate lathe you can soon turn these out of a small, square stick of boxwood. Buy an old two-foot rule and you will have enough boxwood to make all your deadeyes and blocks, too, for the "Sea Witch."

Turn them out so that they are a good 1/16 of an inch thick with a score around the edge to take the wire of the chain-plate, a scant 1/32 of an inch in diameter (Figs. 129 and 134). After making one or two you will learn

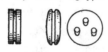

how to roll the file over so as to make the faces of the deadeye slightly rounded and to round off the edges. To strap the

Fig. 129. Deadeyes

deadeyes take a piece of copper, or silver wire, and bend it around in the score, keeping the odd eye down and twist the end of the wire a turn or two around the standing part or long end (Fig. 130).

Fig. 130

As the twisted part is hidden in the channel through which it goes, see that it goes down snug against it by boring a hole large enough to take the twisted portion. This way is good enough on small models. If the model were larger it would look better to make the strapping of the deadeye one piece and hook the chain-plate into it.

As its name signifies these chain-plates were at first made of chain. This, in later years, was made of two, long links, the upper one through the deadeye strap and the lower one ending in an eye for the bolt that held it to the ship's side, the bolts always going through the heavy strakes of the wales (Fig. 131).

In the latter days of sailing
ships, and generally in small vessels that had no channels, but
where the chain-plates were in
the form of flat straps of metal
bolted up the side of the ship, this
strap ended in an eye extending
up through the channel or rail,

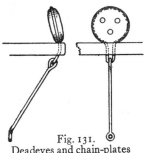

Fig. 131.
Deadeyes and chain-plates

and the strap around the deadeye was either a flat band
(Fig. 132) with an eye at each end through which short
bolts were put, hinging it to the eye of the chain-plate; or
it was round iron doubled, set in a double score around
the deadeye and forming a loop on each side for the connecting bolt to go through (Fig. 133).

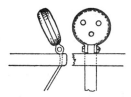

Fig. 132. Flat strapping

Fig. 133. Round strapping

If you have no lathe or access to one, deadeyes can be
turned out quite easily from celluloid knitting needles
that you can generally buy in the 5 and 10 cent stores.
Buy them the diameter you want the deadeyes to be.
You will need smaller sizes also, for the topgallant backstays and for the topmast shrouds when you come to rig
the model.

To work out the deadeyes you will need your pin-vise
with a No. 65 drill and your thin, knife-edge file, a piece
of fine No. 0 or No. 00 sandpaper, and a knife.

Cut off the pointed end of the knitting needle and bore

the three eyes for the deadeye. Then file a score around the needle as close to the edge as you can, a score deep enough to take the wire that is to make the chain-plate. Then file another score beyond that one and with your knife cut off the deadeye (Fig. 134).

Fig. 134

The holes for the lanyards should be carefully bored so that the lanyards will lay, evenly spaced. Be careful to get the two lower ones on a line across the middle of the deadeye and the upper one above so the three holes form a triangle. As all the strain is on upper deadeyes under these holes, there should be more wood left under them than above them and not have the two lower holes away down near the bottom of the deadeye (Fig. 135). Round off a slight score on the under edge of each lanyard hole so that the sharp corner will be taken off and not be left to cut through the lanyard (Fig. 129).

RIGHT

WRONG

Fig. 135

Now bend a piece of copper wire (about 1/32 of an inch in diameter) around the deadeye in the score cut there and twist the wire snugly together, cutting off all surplus end. With the deadeye just flush on its under side with the top of the channel (and be sure they stay down snug), measure your wire down to a good eighth of an inch below the level of the deck and turn in an eye or loop just big enough to let a bank pin go through it. Nail this fast to the hull with the bank pin, leaving the head rounded as it is.

Be careful to get each chain-plate exactly in line with the angle of the shroud it connects with, keeping the line of pins that fasten them to a hull a fair one (Fig. 136). Don't get one up higher than the adjoining one, nor let the deadeyes stick up above the channel too far (Fig.

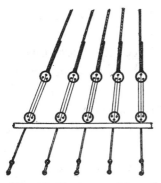

Fig. 136. Deadeyes and shrouds

138). Another important point to look out for is to see that all the deadeyes stand so that the two holes are at right angles to the line of the shroud. Sometimes the deadeyes get slightly turned or canted in the wire loop holding them, so that two holes are about in line with the shroud, which spoils the even lay of the lanyards, and be sure and have the *odd hole up in the upper deadeyes* and *down in the lower deadeyes* on a gang of rigging (Figs. 136 and 137). The center lanyard should show up the longest of the three and not as the shortest.

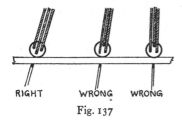

RIGHT   WRONG   WRONG

Fig. 137

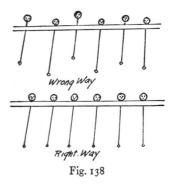

Wrong Way

Right Way

Fig. 138

To make your model look more shippy put a backing link below each chain-plate as follows: Flatten down the eye in the lower end of your chain-plate and then make a short piece of wire into a link with an eye in each end only ⅛ of an inch between the eyes. Flatten the upper one that is to go over the lower eye of the chain-plate and kink it so that the lower eye will come into line with the chain-plate (Fig. 139). This gives more than one bolt for the pull on the shrouds to have to shear before things give way. It's a tedious bit of work, but helps the appearance of the model far-more

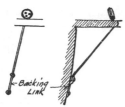

Fig. 139. Backing link

than you would imagine a little thing like that could do.

We have now come to what is the most delicate piece of work about the whole model, so far, and that is the monkey-rail around the poop deck. This is an open, hand-rail, open because it is not boarded up beneath but merely supported on turned stanchions 3/16 of an inch in height (Fig. 140), about every ¾ of an inch apart or 6 feet apart on the real ship.

With a small lathe these stanchions can be turned up out of metal or wood. Metal is preferable, as the putting of pins down through such small stanchions is impractical and to leave a tiny peg-end at top and bottom of each stanchion, to drive into holes bored into the small top-rail and monkey-rail, is most exasperating work because it is so tiny and apt to break just at the wrong time. With metal these peg-ends will have some strength.   I persisted in my "Sea Witch" model, however, and found when it was all on and the glue had set that it had a surprising amount of rigidity.

Across the stern, bore down on the same slant as the transom for a central stanchion, with two on each side of it into the deck waterways, the outer one up in the corner where the side and transom meet.

Fig. 140

Use squared stanchions for these after ones and pull the crown of the rail down at each end with a bank pin driven, not through the outer stanchions, but down alongside of them as that is the way these rails are secured on the real ship. What makes this rail particularly difficult is that it has to slant inboard quite a little.   The stanchions have to be cut on a bevel (Fig. 141) to suit

this and the little peg-end makes this delicate work in
fitting. The monkey-rail should be made of
hard wood. It is only a toothpick in size, any-
way, and where you have to drill holes for the
peg-ends of the stanchions to fit into it there is
great liability of its being broken. It is only
1/16 of an inch wide by a stout 1/32 of an inch
thick. Two pieces each seven inches long will make the
two rails. The piece across the stern had better be cut
to shape and in width left a stout 1/16 of an inch. Halve
the two rails together at the corners and glue them; holding them with one of those wooden, spring "clothes pins"
(Fig. 142) that by sharpening the ends down a little very

Fig. 141

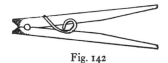

Fig. 142

Fig. 143

often come in handy in model work. They come made
with a slight forked end, but this you can cut down to a
pointed end (Fig. 143).

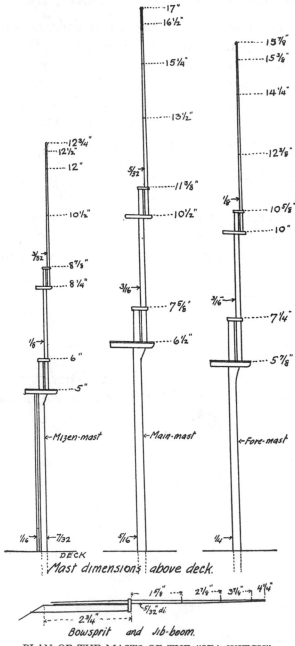

PLAN OF THE MASTS OF THE "SEA WITCH"

CHAPTER X

The Spars

THE picture of a model of the "Sea Witch," the frontispiece of this volume, with the sail plan as a guide, will show clearly how the ship is to be rigged; but the plans of the masts with their dimensions figured in inches, to match the ⅛ inch scale on which the hull is made, will facilitate the work for those not used to working from plans.

These are given for the reason that nine out of ten model makers get their ship spars far too heavy and this fault would be particularly noticeable on a clipper model whose upper spars should look like toothpicks and their ropes aloft like cobwebs. The taper from the stout, heavily rigged lower masts to the tiny skysail yards must be preserved if you want her to look like a clipper.

Make all her spars out of clear, straight-grained white pine, sandpapered and finished with orange shellac. First cut the stick the length the spar requires. With a small plane square it up accurately and then give it the required taper, still keeping it square. After it is so shaped and found to be accurate, plane off the corners, making it eight-sided, finally working it round with a very light shaving off of each edge and finish it round with sandpaper.

Spin it by rubbing one end between your knee and the palm of your hand holding the other end of the spar on sandpaper and you can soon true it up round.

The lower masts have a very slight taper, the mast-heads being squared. Because the parrel strap which holds the topsail yard to the topmast slides up and down as the yard is hoisted and lowered, the topmast generally had so little taper that to all intents and purposes it was a parallel stick and it should be made to carry out this effect.

The top-gallant royal and skysail masts are all in one stick, but should have just the slightest bit of a shoulder at each place where the various gangs of shrouds and stays make fast, to keep them from sliding down the spar and so causing the rigging to slacken.

The yards for this ship are to be made according to the following measurements:

Fore yard .... 8⅜ inches total length; arms ¼ inch each
Fore topsail yard .... 6⅛ " " " " ½ " "
Fore top-gallant yard... 4½ " " " " 3/16 " "
Fore royal yard .... 3½ " " " " ⅛ " "
Fore skysail yard .... 2½ " " " " 1/16 " "
Fore yard studding sail booms........ 4¼ inches long, one on each side
Fore topsail .... 3⅛ " " " " " "
Fore top-gallant .... 2½ " " " " " "
Fore royal .... 1⅝ " " " " " "
Main yard .... 9¼ inches total length; arms ⅝ inch each
Main topsail yard .... 7¼ " " " " ½ " "
Main top-gallant yard 5¾ " " " " ¼ " "
Main royal yard .... 4⅛ " " " " ⅛ " "
Main skysail yard .... 3 " " " " 1/16 " "
Main yard studding sail booms...... 4½ inches long, one on each side
Main topsail .... 3½ " " " " " "
Main top-gallant .... 3 " " " " " "
Main royal .... 2 " " " " " "
Crossjack yard .... 7½ inches total length; arms ½ inch each
Mizzen topsail yard ...... 5¾ " " " " ⅜ " "
Mizzen top-gallant yard 4 " " " " 3/16 " "
Mizzen royal yard .... 3⅛ " " " " ⅛ " "
Mizzen skysail yard ...... 2⅛ " " " " 1/16 " "
Spanker boom .... 6 inches long
Spanker gaff................... 4 3/16 " "

Having the lengths of the yards the utmost importance should be attached to determining the proper diameters for the yards and then being careful to make them conform to those dimensions.

Long experience in making sailing ship spars taught the old shipbuilders what sizes were safe and these have been laid down in often reprinted rules.

Main and fore yards, at the slings or middle, should be seven-tenths of an inch in diameter to every three feet of their length.

Topsail yards, five-sevenths of an inch in diameter to every three feet of length.

Top-gallant yards, six-tenths of an inch in diameter to every three feet of length.

Royal yards, one-half the diameter of the topsail yards.

Skysail yards, two-thirds the diameter of the royal yards.

Studding sail yards, one inch in diameter for every five feet of length.

Studding sail booms, one inch in diameter for every five feet of length.

Jib boom, seven-eighths of an inch in diameter for every three feet of length.

Make your yards so that the diameter at the ends is one-half of what it is at the middle, but do not make the taper of the yards begin at the middle, for about one-third out from the middle, on each side of the yard, should show only a slight trace of diminishing and then the taper increases to the ends. If you divide the yard on each side into quarters, the old ship or spar makers' rule says that the yard at the first quarter division on each side of the mast or middle of the yard should be 30/31 of what it is at the middle.

At the second quarter division, or half way out on the

yard on each side, it should be ⅞ of what it is at the middle. At the third quarter division, 7/10; and at the end, 3/7 of its diameter at the middle.

Use these rules in proportioning your yards. To give them here in figures would require a micrometer to get the minute graduations. Once learn the rule, and carefully following it, make one spar and you will catch on to the proper taper for a yard and your model will look much better for the time and study you have put into these details.

RIVER SCHOONER

CHAPTER XI

TOOLS FOR MODEL MAKING

THE old sailor, far out at sea on a ship, with only a jackknife to work with and maybe a needle or two out of which to improvise drills, worked under disadvantages in making his ship model. With us there are a number of tools that greatly facilitate model building and we will consider them in rotation, in about the way they will be required.

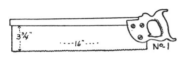

Fig. 144. Panel saw

The panel or back saw (Fig. 144) will, in most cases, suffice for the cutting of the block when starting to shape the hull out of a block of wood; although, if the model is going to be a very large one, an ordinary cross-cut saw, without the back, which limits the depth of cut the saw can make to about four inches, is preferable for sawing the block to approximate shape.

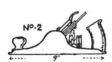

Fig. 145. Block plane

An iron block plane (Fig. 145), a smoothing plane, is often needed in smoothing boards for making a perfect joint between them.

Fig. 146. Drawknife

A drawknife (Fig. 146) is very valuable in commencing to shape up the block at the start, to rough out the bottom and sides, though this can be dispensed with and the same work done at the expense of a little more labor with a chisel and a plane.

Fig. 147. Chisel

At least one good-sized chisel (Buck's bevelled-edge, socket chisel) is essential (Fig. 147). You can get a much better control over a large chisel in cutting out the hull. It is more desirable than a smaller one. The size and weight of the chisel give accuracy not found in a small, light one.

Fig. 148. Gouge

For the same reason as in the case of the chisel, the control, lessened liability to slip and cut yourself, makes a good-sized gouge (Fig. 148) an indispensable tool when you come to hollow out the inside of the model.

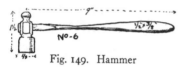

Fig. 149. Hammer

The hammer question is much the same as choosing a fountain pen. Get one that hangs comfortably in your hand. A small hammer, such as is here illustrated (Fig. 149), is about the size needed for most of the work done on models. Once in a great while, in starting to put the block together, an ordinary sized, large hammer, such as nearly every family is provided with, may be needed.

Fig. 150
Block plane

A small, iron block plane (Fig. 150) about 1¼ inches wide, of this type will be found invaluable all through the process of model making and you can generally buy them in a five and ten cent store, as good as is needed. The only thing required with any plane and with any other tool, too, for that matter, is to keep the blade sharp.

Fig. 151. Gouge-shaped plane

This plane (Fig. 151), only about ½ inch wide, with a gouge-shaped blade, is sold by musical instrument makers. The handle fits into the hollow of your hand and you hold the little metal plane between thumb and fore finger and for moulding the after part of your ship model it is a very valuable tool to have. You can get into places where no other tool seems to fit.

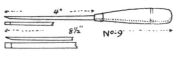

Fig. 152. Chisels

Two small chisels (Fig. 152), one ⅛ of an inch wide at the cutting edge and one 3/16 or ¼ of an inch, are handy in many ways.

This little bent chisel (Fig. 153) is one of a set of six wood carving tools sold by the Millers Falls Company and is about the most valuable chisel of all for model work. With it you can cut into places where no straight chisel will work. Of the rest of the set, the ordinary straight chisel and small gouge are also very useful; but the V-shaped gouge and

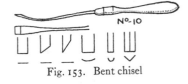

Fig. 153. Bent chisel

the others are seldom needed. You have to take the whole set in purchasing.

As you advance in model making you will find it convenient to get small pieces of steel wire and grind the

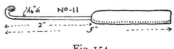

Fig. 154

ends down to make small chisels to suit the work in hand. Sometimes it is necessary to bend this wire into a hook shape (Fig. 154), so that it is like a surgeon's lance, and make a small wooden handle to stick the shank end into, in order to reach up in under places and make cuttings.

This is a regular stock panel saw (Fig. 155) made for fine cutting by Henry Disston & Sons, of Philadelphia, and it is the most useful saw in model making. But there are times, when making small hatch coaming-bitts, etc., for the deck furnishings on the model, where this saw,

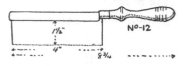

Fig. 155. Panel saw

with its 32 teeth to the inch, would butcher the work irreparably and so in order to get a saw fine enough to do the work you will have to make a holder just like a panel or back saw, by taking a piece of thin brass and bending it over to form a slot in which to hold the saw blade and then drive the end into a small

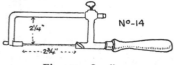

Fig. 156. Fine hack saw

wooden handle. The blades for this saw (Fig. 156) are made from a hack saw blade that has about 64 teeth to the inch and has teeth on both edges; and when one edge becomes worn out you can remove the blade from the back and reverse it. A saw of this kind will cut quick and clean and so fine you can hardly see the cut it makes.

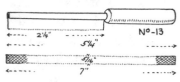

Fig. 157. Scroll saw

A very fine scroll saw (Fig. 157) to cut out the curved pieces, either a hand saw, such as here illustrated, or a power saw will do. If you are going to build up the model, frame by frame, just as a real ship is constructed, some form of power jig saw is to be preferred.

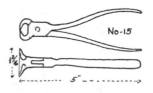

Fig. 158. Pliers

In the matter of pliers you need a good pair of cutting pliers, either the square ended kind (Fig. 158), here shown, or a pair of those where the cutting edge is set on a bevel. Either will do, so long as you have a cutting end that projects so you can reach into close corners and cut off nails or pins.

Fig. 159. Long-nosed pliers

A pair of long-nosed pliers (Fig. 159) does what your fingers are too clumsy to do and will reach in where you could not. The jaws come flat together, but they should be rounded on the backs for bending loops and eyes in wire and pins.

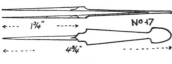

Fig. 160. Tweezers

Tweezers (Fig. 160), for picking up small pins and countless other jobs, are a companion as valuable as the jackknife.

After all, the jackknife (Fig. 161) is the main tool in model work and one we shall not try to recommend. All you need to get is a good one, of steel that will hold an edge and the sooner the blade wears down to the shape shown in the sketch the more useful you will find it. Some

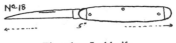

Fig. 161. Jackknife

men get a piece of tool steel and grind it to a shape to suit their fancy. Some take a piece of an old hack saw blade (made of highly tempered steel) and grind that to a blade to suit, wrapping on a handle of adhesive tape. Then there is a knife whose handle is a chuck (Fig. 162) into which any one of three blades may be inserted or removed by twisting the handle, which opens the chuck jaws that hold the blade.

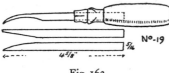

Fig. 162

But in using a knife, or any wood-cutting tool, for that matter, keep your oil stones handy and just rub them lightly occasionally and you will get better results than in waiting until it gets real dull.

Drills come far too large for any model work. The largest you will ever need will be those with which to bore the mast holes or about ½ of an inch in diameter. But as to smallness there is a limit. No. 80 is the smallest. It drills a hole far too fine for a bank pin to go into, and No. 75 is about as small as you will ever need. There are a few intermediate sizes, No. 70, No. 65, etc., up to about No. 40. Small chucks called pin-vise (Fig. 163) to hold these drills, knurled and round so that you can spin them between your thumb and fore finger to drill small holes with, may be purchased at tool stores, and it pays to have more than one.

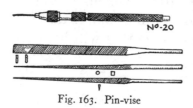

Fig. 163. Pin-vise

A set of small files, known as die sinkers, comprising about nine different shapes of blades, will be found indispensable in model work. Some are three cornered, some oval shaped blades, but the five here shown are by far the most useful. A small flat file with round-cutting edges, the sides of which are smooth, a tapered, square file, a tapered, round (or rat-tail) file and a knife-blade file that comes to a knife edge that cuts, with a very thin back to it; these files are really all one needs in the smaller sizes.

For shaping the hull, a ten or twelve inch, flat half-round and round file, rather coarse cut, but not a rasp, will be of great assistance in finishing up doing the work, better than sandpaper and with more precision than a cutting tool.

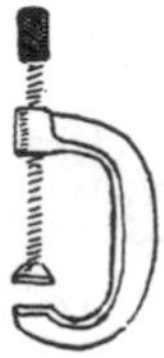

In the matter of holding-on implements, a small, metal vise (Fig. 164) that you can clamp on to a table top, is wanted; a few assorted sizes of five and ten cent store metal screw clamps;

Fig. 164

[165] CLIPPER SHIP "SEA WITCH," BUILT IN 1846, IN NEW YORK

From the oil painting by Charles Robert Patterson

and also a few wooden, spring clips or clothes pins which, by cutting off the blunt ends to a point, make a most useful clamp with which to hold glued pieces together, where only a light pressure is required.

Pinky, Fishing Schooner

CHAPTER XII

Glossary

Abaft — Towards the stern or rear of the ship.

Aft — Towards the stern or rear end of a ship.

After-body — That part of the ship's hull that is aft of the middle.

Amidships — The middle part of a ship — more often pronounced 'midships. In naval architecture the widest or bulkiest part of the ship is called the midship section and designated by a scroll symbol. This in ships was always a little forward of the mid-length of the ship.

Anchor — A heavy iron hook used to hold a ship stationery in shallow water.

Athwartship — Across the ship.

Backing Link — A link of iron added below the chainplate on a ship to give added strength.

Backstays — Ropes leading well aft from the top of a mast to prevent its being pulled forward.

Belaying Pin — An iron or hard wood pin used to twist rope about so as to hold the ropes.

Bilge — In speaking of the shape of a ship it refers to the corner where the bottom and sides meet, being an "easy bilge" or a "hard bilge" as the radius of the arc forming the bilge is long or short. Aboard ship the bilge, as generally referred to, is the inside of the ship's bottom between the outside planking and the inside ceiling, where bilge water collects.

Bitts — Wooden or iron posts, generally in pairs, around which the mooring lines or anchor cables are made fast. At the foot of each mast on deck, bitts are placed to take the heavy strain of the topsail sheets.

BOOBY HATCH — A light, portable, box-like cover that is lashed over the after hatch and gives access below through a small companionway slide in the top of it.

BOW — The forward end of the ship. As there are two sides to it they are generally referred to as the bows: "Off the starboard bow," "Off the port bow," "Under the bows," etc. We speak of a ship as being very "bluff bowed" or "can bowed."

BOWSPRIT — The spar that sticks out at the forward end of the ship.

BOWSPRIT CAP — At the outer end of the bowsprit is a heavy block of wood with a hole cut through it for the jib-boom to slide out and in on top of the bowsprit. A strap of iron around this cap strengthens it.

BULL'S EYES — Round, flattened pieces of hard wood or lignum-vitæ, having one large hole through, with three ridges at one end to take the rope lashings put through and quite similar to a deadeye.

BULWARKS — The fence-like structure raised along the sides of a vessel to prevent things from falling off.

BUMPKIN — A short timber or iron projecting out from the side of a ship — as the main-brace bumpkin — fitted away aft on a ship to keep the brace out clear of the mizzen rigging.

BUNG DIPPER — A small vessel used to dip up water from a barrel through the bung-hole.

CABLES — Are either of chain or hemp. If chain, they have a small strut called a stud that keeps the two sides of a link apart and prevents the link flattening under a heavy strain. If of hemp or manilla, the cable consists of three smaller rope twisted so that the strands lay just the opposite to the way the strands of the rope are laid up.

CAMBRE OR CROWN — The up-curve of the deck beams from side to side of the ship which causes the water to drain off.

CAPSTAN — A round, vertical spool, on a ship's deck, for winding in ropes, a powerful leverage being obtained by the use of long bars inserted in the top of the capstan head by which it is turned.

CASKS — Stout barrels used for carrying water on a ship.

CAT-FALLS — A tackle rove through sheaves set vertically in the outer end of the cat-head and through a large, strong block below called the cat-block.

CAT-HEADS — Short, strong timbers projecting from the bluff part of a ship's bows and used for hoisting up the anchor.

CAT-HOOK — A large, iron hook used to hook around the anchor in hoisting it up onto the ship's deck.

CAVIL — A stout cleat of wood bolted fore and aft on the inside of the bulwark stanchions around which heavy ropes may be wound and so secured.

CHAIN-PLATES — Iron rods bolted to the ship's side below the channels that hook into the iron straps of the deadeyes.

CHANNELS — Wide boards which spread the chain-plates far enough out from the ship's side so that the shrouds will not touch the ship's rail above as they slant inboard to the masthead.

CHOCKS — Metal scores or notch-shaped castings for ropes to run through, their upper edges having horn-like projections that prevent the ropes from slipping out when once they are put into the chock and yet open enough at the top to permit the rope being removed.

CLIPPER SHIP — A vessel cut away so sharp in the ends that carrying capacity is sacrificed for the speed so attained.

COACH-HOUSE — A sort of vestibule built at the forward entrance to the cabin.

COMPANIONWAY — The entrance to the cabin or living quarters of a ship.

COPPER — The entire outside of the ship's hull from just above the water level clear down to and including the keel was covered with thin sheets of copper to keep off the growth of weeds and barnacles and to preserve the wood against the destructive wood-boring teredo.

COUNTER — The overhanging part of the after end of a ship above the water.

CROWN. See CAMBRE.

DAVITS — Timbers erected as derricks for hoisting in anchors or boats along a ship's side or over the stern. Iron davits later succeeded the clumsy wooden ones. Some ships carried their side-lights on a pair of light iron davits swung out aft, on each side of the stern.

DEADEYES — Flat, round discs of hard wood, generally lignum-vitæ, with a groove or score cut around the outside in which the shrouds are bent and siezed fast, with three holes in a triangle, their lower ends rounded so as not to break the lanyards which hold them.

DECK — The floors upon which the men walk. To make them shed water readily they are slightly arched from side to side of the ship and drain holes, called scuppers, are fitted through the side of the ship to carry off the water.

Decks are usually a little thicker than the side planking to allow for the continual wear they are subjected to.

They are many narrow planks laid lengthwise of the ship with their seams caulked, or made water-tight with threads of oakum hammered down into each seam and the remaining part of each seam, for half an inch or so in depth, filled with melted pitch in the older ships, and with a patented seam composition that never absolutely hardens but stays just pliable enough, like rubber, to contract and expand as the wood expands or contracts in hot or cold weather, and so keeps the water from filtering through the deck and spoiling the cargo.

In older ships where they curled up excessively at the ends, the decks did not sweep up so much, making only a moderate rise at the two ends. An experiment was once made by laying the decks in a level plane fore and aft; but when the ship heeled over on one side, it was found that all the water flowed forward or aft and flooded the living quarters.

DECK BUCKETS — Small wooden buckets fitted with rope handles used principally in washing down the decks.

DECK FURNITURE — A general name for all deck super-structures, such as houses, bitts, ladders, etc.

DRAFT — The depth of water required to float the ship.

DRAW BUCKET — A bucket made of canvas, like a bag, its mouth held open by a rope grommet or iron ring and used in dipping up water from over the side.

DUMB-BRACE — A metal shoulder fitted on the stern-post for one of the rudder pintles to bear on.

FIGUREHEAD — A carved image fastened to the top of the stem or knee of the head.

FISH-TACKLE — A strong tackle from the fore-topmast head used to hoist the anchors up onto the ship's forecastle head or deck.

FLARE OR FLAM — That part of the ship's side at the bows that extends out so it overhangs the water more than the part below it.

FORE FOOT — The lower end of the stem where it and the forward end of the keel meet. Also referred to as the gripe.

FORECASTLE — The crew's living space, formerly built away up in the bows of the ship, below decks. About 1830 these quarters were provided in a house built on deck just behind the foremast and were dryer and better ventilated quarters.

FORECASTLE HEAD — The raised deck built across the forward end of a ship.

FORWARD — Towards the front of the ship.

FREEBOARD — The height of the side of the ship remaining above water after she is loaded.

FREEING-PORTS — Large, square hinged openings in the main bulwarks of the ship that were left free to swing open and drain the decks when the waves flooded the decks in bad weather.

GALLEY — The kitchen on a ship. On large old-time men-of-war, it used to be away down in the bottom of the ship, in the middle. Later it was placed under the upper deck just behind the foremast. On ships having a forecastle built on deck, the galley generally occupies the after part of this house. Small vessels had a portable, box-like structure that was lashed on deck or on top of the main hatch after the ship was loaded.

GANGWAY — A passageway cut through the side of the ship to permit more ready entrance to the deck. On men-of-war it was a narrow deck extending along the side connecting the raised deck aft with the forecastle head.

GINGERBREAD-WORK — A sea term meaning a lot of unnecessary panel work or ornamental work.

GRATINGS — Thin strips of hardwood laid, with intervals between them, across heavier strips spaced so that square holes are left and used to prevent a man from falling down a hatchway and yet to permit air to circulate below. Also laid on deck, as at the wheel, or gangway, like a door-mat, to take the wear off the deck and yet allow free drainage of water below.

GROMMET — A small ring made of cord or rope.

GUDGEONS — Metal fittings riveted to the stern-post and having holes to receive the pintles of the rudder.

HAND ROPES — Ropes hanging down on each side of a ladder to assist one in climbing up — like the balistrades on a stairway.

HATCH OR HATCHWAY — Openings in a ship's deck through which the cargo is lowered into the inside.

HATCH BARS — Iron strips laid across the top of the hatch to hold the tarpaulins down tight.

HATCH-BATTENS — Iron strips wedged tightly against the tarpaulins put over the hatches around each side of the hatch coaming.

HATCH-COAMING — Raised, box-like sides around the hatches to keep out the water.

HATCH-COVERS — The hatches are closed by heavy sections of the deck cut into small squares so that they can be lifted off. When the ship is loaded these covers are put in place and the joints caulked and sealed with hot pitch poured into them like the rest of the deck, to keep out water.

HAWSE-HOLES — Holes through the ship's bows through which the anchor cables lead. When hemp cables were used, several thicknesses of wood were imposed one on top of another so as to pad them out and make the corner of the rope bent over as easy and as large a radius as possible in order to prevent breaking the fibres of the cable and to make it easier to drag the rope over while heaving in the cable.

HOLY-STONES — Pieces of sandstone, about eight inches square, used with sand to grind the surface of the decks smooth and clean.

KEEL — The square timber along the bottom of the ship.

KNEE — A piece of wood cut from a tree where the trunk or limbs fork out at an angle, so that the natural grain of the wood is similar to the angular shape of the knee.

LADDERS — Ladders were fitted to ascend to the various decks on a ship. When anchored in harbor, the ship's gangway ladder — a platform above and one below close to the water connected by a long pair of steps — was generally put into place, the lower end raised and lowered to the desired height by a tackle from an iron davit above.

At sea, when taking a pilot aboard, a rope ladder would be thrown over, the oak rungs of which were set into ovals of wood and a succession of these strung on to ropes down each side.

LANYARDS — Small ropes that lace the upper and lower deadeyes together. By tightening up on this lacing the shrouds that steady the mast heads are set up tight or "taut," as sailors term it.

LAZARETTE — The ship's store-room away aft at the stern abaft the transoms.

LIGHT-BOARDS — Vertical boards placed behind the lanterns that are called the side-lights, so as to form a screen whereby the lights will only show ahead and also out off the side on which they are placed.

MASTS — The large, upright spars that carry the sails of the ship. A ship has three masts, although in later years — 1880 on — ships have been built with four or five masts. There were a few in olden times that had more than three masts. The forward one is called the foremast; the middle one the mainmast and the after one the mizzenmast. When another was added it became known as the jiggermast and the fifth one was the drivermast.

MONKEY RAIL — The term given to the upper, fence-like rail around the quarter-deck of a ship.

PAYED — The seams of the planking and deck are payed by wiping or pouring full of hot pitch to seal the seams so the caulking will not work out, and also to help to keep them water-tight.

PENNANT — A piece of strong, tarred rope used to shorten up the length of a brace by bringing the blocks closer together.

PINTLE — The straps on the rudder that carry the pins that fit into the holes of the gudgeons on the stern-post and so form hinges on which the rudder swings.

PLANKING LINES — Shipbuilders took great pride in seeing that all the seams of the planks made fair, graceful sweeps or curves at all angles at which they might be viewed. The rounded and hollowed shape of the ship called for much ingenuity in laying out the belts of planking so that no sudden bends became apparent on going from end to end of the ship over the various forms the ship's side assumes throughout its length.

POOP DECK — The after part of the main deck away back near the stern. When there was a raised deck aft it was called the poop deck. The highest raised deck aft.

PRAYER BOOKS — Small pieces of sandstone, about four inches square and six inches long, used to grind the deck smooth in small corners where the holystones cannot go.

PUMPS — The history of ship's pumps would of itself form a good sized book. About every known means of raising water has been tried at various times on board a ship, from the common wood-box pump to the double-acting Deluge pump. Men-of-war, about the time of American Revolution, used the endless chain pump and the amount of water they could discharge was prodigious. I once saw an account of how many tons of water they could discharge in a moment but I cannot just now locate it. But when you consider that the crank arms which turned the sprocket wheels, over which the chain with its many suckers turned, were extended fore and aft on the gun-deck far enough to permit about a dozen husky men-of-warsmen to lay hold of them, it may be true. Merchantmen, about this time, had single-acting plunger pumps with athwartships pump brakes enabling about four men on each side to get hold and pump. This continued until about 1840, when the flywheel pump, with a short lift but large diameter of plunger or diaphragm, came into use with many other improvements and this is what the "Sea Witch" carried.

QUARTER-BADGE — The timber fitted up and down over the after ends of the side planking that was shaped to carry the sides of the transoms out in a neat curve, thereby relieving the square, box-like appearance the transom would otherwise have.

QUARTER-DECK — The after, raised deck reserved for the use of the ship's officers.

QUARTER-GALLERIES — The "Sea Witch" had none, but nearly every old ship, prior to and a few after 1800, had a kind of little overhanging bay-window on each side, away aft, ending against the quarter-badge. These beveled windows, with their carved, ornamental work, added much to the picturesqueness of the older ships.

QUARTERS — The sides of the ship, away aft, that ended at the transom or back end of the ship.

RABBET LINE — The seam where all the planking on the outside of the ship joins the central portion of the ship; composed of the keel, the stem, the stern-post and the transom.

RAILS — Thin, beaded strips that extended from bow to stern outlining the ship's sheer. The finish piece on top of the bulwarks. Thin strips inside the bulwarks projecting out far enough to carry the belaying pins on which the ship's ropes were made fast. Also the pin-rails around each mast, supported, off the deck, on turned stanchions, where belaying pins were fitted. At the bow, on old-time, frigate-built ships, several narrow strips known as the hair-rail, middle-rail, bracket-rail, etc., acted as braces to steady the figurehead.

RANGE — The range of the deck is referred to often in old books and means the clear space from end to end on the decks.

RING BOLTS — Bolts fastened to some part of the ship having a ring in top into which blocks may be hooked or lashings made to hold something from shifting.

RUDDER — The vertical timbers hinged to the after end of the ship — to its stern-post — by which the ship is turned.

RUDDER-COAT — A tarred, canvas covering nailed to the stern of the ship and to the rudder with slack enough to permit the latter to swing, put there to keep the water from splashing up through the large opening necessary on the old style, rule-joint hung rudders.

RUDDER-HEAD — The upper part of the rudder that extends up into the stern of the ship and into which the tiller is fitted.

RUDDER-STOCK — The head and its continuation down forming the principle timber on which the rest of the rudder is built.

RUN — The after, underwater portion of the ship.

SADDLES — Wooden bearers under water-casks, cut to fit the shape of the casks. Saddles on spars are short projections fastened on a mast to prevent a boom or similar spar from slipping down.

SAILING LIGHTS OR SIDELIGHTS — These came into vogue about 1850, the navigation laws being revised to compel all ships to carry a green lantern on the starboard side and a red lantern on the port side, so that a vessel meeting her could tell which way she was heading. Prior to that date, a single, white lantern was carried on the cap of the bowsprit and it was a guess which way the ship might be sailing.

SCARPH — The joining of two timbers by lapping and so beveling the lapped part so that the timber is of one uniform, continuous size.

SCUPPERS — Drains to carry off water. The main deck scuppers were large lead pipes, flanged flush with the deck, leading down and out through the ship's sides where they were flanged flush with the planking. The scuppers draining from one deck to another and off the tops of deck-houses always had the lead pipe sticking down and out, away from the sides, so that the water would drip clear and not slobber down and stain the white paint.

SHEATHING — The protecting covering of boards or copper nailed outside on a ship's bottom. The boards that enclose the sides of the deck forming the bulwarks on the outside of the ship and the bulkheads at the forward end of the raised after-deck. Boards forming the inside skin or lining of a ship over her frames.

SHEER — The rise towards each end. Some ships have considerable so that the ends are much higher above the water than the ship is in the middle and others have a rather straight sheer.

SHROUDS — Tarred ropes that hold the masts in place.

SKID-BEAMS — Light timbers on which the life boats are stowed.

SKYLIGHTS — Box-like structures on deck to admit air and light into the cabins below. Most American ships had flat-topped skylights with sliding or hinged windows in the sides. Men-of-war often had the flat, inverted V top skylights, the glass protected by iron or brass rods. Circular skylights made this way were much in vogue in the navy about 1840.

SNI — A crook or curve in a plank or spar; something out of a straight line or fair curve.

SOOGY-MOOGY — A strong alkaline used to wash off painted woodwork.

STANCHIONS — Uprights supporting the bulwarks along the ship's sides (also called timber-heads). Uprights supporting the pin-rails around the masts; also upright props between the decks, inside the ship.

STEERING WHEELS — These became necessary as ships increased in size and the tiller, with its tackle, became cumbersome. The leverage attained by a wheel, over the tiller ropes wound around a small barrel, enabled one or two men to do what four to six men were formerly needed for. As long as wooden tillers were used, which was up to about 1800, the steering wheels were placed over the forward end of this huge timber which traveled across the ship close up under the deck beams, supported on timbers and pulled either way by tackles rove off to each side of the ship, the hauling ends coming to the middle oversheaves and so up and around the drum or barrel of the steering wheel. Big three-deckers and even large frigates had double-steering wheels, so four men could get hold of and keep control of the steering gear. But the introduction of short, iron tillers permitted their being fitted abaft the rudder head and this moved the steering wheel away aft. Ships began to be so fitted about 1820 or a trifle later.

STEEVE — The upward inclination of a spar above the horizontal.

STEM — The forward edge of the ship; a vertical member.

STERN-POST — The vertical member at the after end of the ship to which the rudder is hinged.

STRAKES — Meaning boards. Each continuous line of boards in a ship's planking is termed a strake of planking.

STRONG BACK — Each large hatchway was subdivided into two parts by a heavy timber fitting into jogs cut in the forward and after faces of the hatch coaming — its upper edge rabbetted for the hatch-covers the same as the adjoining coamings.

TARPAULINS — Tar soaked canvas used as waterproof coverings over hatchways or for coverings of any deck work.

TAUT — Tight.

TILLERS — The first primitive way of controlling the rudder and still used on small vessels. All vessels still have some sort of tillers with which to give the necessary leverage to turn the rudder, but tillers are now controlled by tackles and steering wheels (see STEERING WHEEL).

TIMBER-HEADS — The extension of the frames above the deck to form the sides of the ship, known as the bulwarks (see STANCHIONS).

TOP-SIDES — That part of a ship which is above the water.

TRANSOM — The flat portion of the ship at the after-end above the stern-post.

TUMBLE-HOME — The rounding in, or swell of a ship's side, making her narrower at the top than she is below.

TURK'S HEAD — A fancy knot that forms a ball on the end of a rope.

Vangs — A pennant and light tackle from the gaff end to each side of the ship to prevent the gaffs swinging about.

Wales — A thick belt of planking extending vertically down below the main deck waterways, the depth depending on the proportions of the ship.

Water-line — Where the surface of the water makes contact with the ship's hull.

Waterways — Around the outer edge of the ship's deck, a heavy, horizontal belt of timber, much thicker than the deck, is built and this extends inboard two to three feet.

Wheel-box — A box built over the steering wheel drum to keep the wheel-rope or tiller-ropes, dry.

Winches — Along in the 1840's further help was given the sailor, when economy demanded a reduction in the number of men in a ship's crew, by the introduction aboard ship of geared-up hand winches, fitted to the topsail-sheet bitts at the forward side of each mast.

Windlass — The windlass, like the pumps, has a long history behind it. Before chain cables came into general use, hemp cables were used, and as this kind of rope was too stiff to bend around a sharp curve the windlasses used to heave it in were huge, log-like affairs extending horizontally across the deck and turned by heavers, wooden levers about six feet long, that were inserted into holes in the windlass and shifted into others as the windlass turned.

Men-of-war used capstans around which, with its many radiating capstan bars, twenty to thirty men could push their way winding in a small rope called a messenger — an endless loop of rope that was fitted with many small tail-ropes — which, as many as could be, were frapped around the cable, being let go as they approached the capstan and others behind being made fast as soon as the cable's coming in permitted, the huge, stiff cable, as thick as a man's leg, being passed below and coiled down in the cable tiers amidships on each side of the ship. It was dangerous work handling such rope — to bitt it — that is, to hitch it to the riding bitts on the deck so as to hold the ship, plunging and jumping in a gale of wind, and yet not get it jammed so that it could be removed.

The invention of the modern windlass, with its wildcat releasing gear, permits the chain cable to run out from the locker down in the fore peak without a man having to touch it and yet one man can turn the wildcat and put on a brake that will stop and hold that chain at any time. To get the chain in again — all hands formerly took hold of heavers fitted to two long, pump arms extending across the forecastle head, and by the leverage so gained, ratcheted the chain in again, link by link, quite rapidly. By applying a worm-gear at the base of a vertical capstan, engaging into a gear on the barrel of the windlass, still another improvement in ground-tackle was made, and men could exert more power with less fatigue by walking around and pushing on a capstan bar.

When the anchor was "up and down" and the big anchor hooked deep into a clay bottom had to be broken out, a process necessitating the whole weight of the ship being thrown against the cable by the use of her sails, still another invention, the double-acting or geared capstan, came into use and further aided the seamen. By shifting their capstan bars into an upper row of holes, and reversing their way around the capstan, double the power was produced to heave in the chain and the anchor came home.

WOOD-LOCK — A block of hard wood fitted below the upper pintle to prevent the rudder from floating up and unhooking itself from the stern-post.

MERRIMACK RIVER GUNDALO

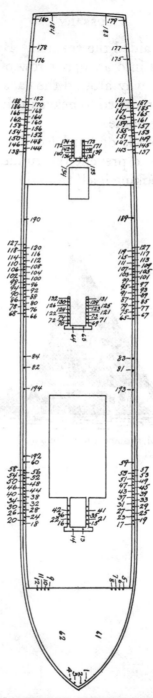

BELAYING PIN LAYOUT ON CLIPPER SHIP "SEA WITCH"

BELAYING PIN LAYOUT ON CLIPPER SHIP "SEA WITCH"

1	Down haul—flying jib.
2	Down haul—inner jib.
3	Down haul—fore top-mast staysail.
4	Down haul—outer jib.
5	Sheets—flying jib.
6	Sheets—outer jib.
7	Sheets—inner jib.
8	Sheets—fore topmast staysail.
9	Sheets—fore topmast staysail.
10	Sheets—inner jib.
11	Sheets—outer jib.
12	Sheets—flying jib.
13 14	Fore topsail sheets.
15 16	Fore yard lifts.
17	Flying jib halliard.
18	Outer jib halliard.
19	Inner jib halliard.
20	Fore topmast staysail halliard.
21 22	Fore clew garnets.
23 24	Fore course reef-tackles.
25 26	Fore course inner buntlines.
27 28	Fore course outer buntlines.
29 30	Fore course leech lines.
31 32	Fore topsail reef tackles.
33 34	Fore topsail buntlines.
35 36	Fore topgallant sheets.
37 38	Fore topsail clew lines.
39 40	Fore topgallant sail clewlines.
41	Main topmast staysail downhaul.
42	Main topgallant mast staysail downhaul.
43 44	Fore topgallant buntlines.
45 46	Fore royal sheets.
47 48	Fore royal clewline.
49 50	Fore royal buntline.
51 52	Fore skysail sheets.
53 54	Fore skysail clewlines.
55	Fore topsail halliard.
56	Fore topgallant sail halliard.
57	Fore royal halliard.
58	Fore skysail halliard.
59 60	Fore sheets.
61 62	Fore course tacks.
63 64	Main topsail sheets.
65	Main topgallant staysail halliard.
66	Main topmast staysail halliard.
67	Main royal staysail halliard.
68	Spare.
69 70	Main yard lifts.

71 72	Main clew garnets.
73 74	Main topsail sheets.
75 76	Fore topgallant yard braces.
77 78	Fore royal yard braces.
79 80	Fore skysail yard braces.
81 82	Fore yard braces.
83 84	Fore topsail yard braces.
85 86	Main course reef tackles.
87 88	Main course inner buntlines.
89 90	Main course outer buntlines.
91 92	Main course leechlines.
93 94	Main topsail reef tackles.
95 96	Main topsail buntlines.
97 98	Main topgallant sail sheets.
99 100	Main topsail clewlines.
101 102	Main topsail buntlines.
103	Mizzen topgallant staysail downhaul.
104	Mizzen topmast staysail downhaul.
105 106	Main royal sheets.
107 108	Main royal clewlines.
109 110	Main royal buntlines.
111 112	Main skysail sheets.
113 114	Main skysail clewlines.
115 116	Main skysail buntlines.
117	Main topgallant sail halliard.
118	Main topsail halliard.
119	Main skysail halliard.
120	Main royal halliard.
121	Mizzen topgallant staysail downhaul.
122	Mizzen topmast staysail downhaul.
123 124	Mizzen topsail yard braces.
125 126	Cro-jack braces.
127 128	Mizzen topgallant yard braces.
129 130	Mizzen royal yard braces.
131 132	Mizzen skysail yard braces.
133 134	Mizzen topsail sheets.
135 136	Cro-jack lifts.
137	Mizzen staysail halliard.
138	Mizzen topmast staysail halliard.
139	Spare.
140	Spare.
141 142	Mizzen topgallant sheets.
143 144	Main topgallant yard braces.

145
146 } Main royal yard braces.

147
148 } Main skysail-yard braces.

149
150 } Mizzen topsail reef-tackles.

151
152 } Mizzen topsail clewlines.

153
154 } Mizzen topsail buntlines.

155
156 } Mizzen topgallant sheets.

157
158 } Mizzen topgallant clewlines.

159
160 } Mizzen topgallant buntlines.

161
162 } Mizzen royal sheets.

163
164 } Mizzen royal clewlines.

165
166 } Mizzen royal buntlines.

167
168 } Mizzen skysail sheets.

169
170 } Mizzen skysail clewlines.

171   Spanker throat-halliards.

172   Spanker peak-halliards.

173
174 } Spanker quarter lifts.

175
176 } Main yard braces.

177
178 } Main topsail yard braces.

179
180 } Spanker sheets.

181
182 } Spanker vangs.

183
184 } Spanker ringtail guys.

185   Mizzen topsail halliard.

186   Mizzen topgallant sail halliard.

187   Mizzen royal halliard.

188   Mizzen skysail halliard.

189
190 } Main course sheets.

191
192 } Main course tacks.

193
194 } Fore course sheets.

Mould No.	MAIN HEIGHT above 7 W.L.	TOP HEIGHT above 7 W.L.	RAIL HEIGHT above 7 W.L.	MAIN HALF BREADTH	TOP HALF BREADTH	RAIL HALF BREADTH	Mould No.	HALF BREADTH 1 W.L.	HALF BREADTH 2 W.L.	HALF BREADTH 3 W.L.	HALF BREADTH 4 W.L.	HALF BREADTH 5 W.L.	HALF BREADTH 6 W.L.	HALF BREADTH 7 W.L.
∞	3-8-4	7-3-0	11-0-4	16-6-0	16-6-0	16-3-0	∞	8-7-1	12-3-2	14-1-5	15-2-0	15-9-5	16-1-6	16-4-1
4	3-6-6	7-2-2	10-8-3	16-5-6	16-5-5	16-2-5	4	8-2-0	11-10-1	13-10-0	15-0-0	15-8-1	16-1-0	16-3-5
8	3-5-5	7-1-3	10-9-2	16-0-5	16-4-0	16-0-2	8	7-2-7	10-10-2	13-0-0	14-4-1	15-2-1	15-8-4	16-0-2
12	3-5-6	7-1-0	10-8-6	15-11-6	16-1-4	15-8-6	12	6-1-0	9-4-5	11-8-0	13-2-0	14-2-3	14-11-0	15-6-0
16	3-7-2	7-2-0	10-9-0	15-6-0	15-10-4	15-6-4	16	4-10-0	7-8-2	9-0-0	11-6-0	12-9-0	13-9-0	14-6-2
20	3-10-0	7-3-6	10-9-4	14-9-0	15-6-0	15-2-6	20	3-6-4	5-9-1	7-7-4	9-2-7	10-8-0	11-11-4	13-1-0
24	4-2-4	7-6-4	10-11-0	13-8-2	14-11-5	14-10-5	24	3-4-3	3-0-0	5-1-7	6-5-5	7-0-0	9-3-0	10-8-0
28	4-5-4	7-10-0	11-1-4	12-0-0	14-3-2	14-5-1	28	1-2-6	1-11-0	2-7-4	3-4-7	4-3-2	5-4-2	6-9-4
30	5-0-4	8-0-6	11-3-0	10-7-0	13-0-4	14-2-0	30	0-8-0	1-0-3	1-5-0	1-10-0	2-4-2	3-0-2	4-1-2
32	5-5-0	8-3-0	11-4-4	8-1-0	13-5-5	13-10-5	32			0-3-0	0-4-6	0-6-2	0-8-6	1-0-0
Cross Seam	5-8-0	8-4-6	11-5-6	7-5-0	13-2-4	13-8-4	Cross Seam							
D	3-9-6	7-6-5	11-3-6	16-4-0	16-4-4	16-4-2	D	8-4-5	11-10-2	13-7-5	14-8-4	15-4-4	15-9-4	16-0-6
H	4-2-0	7-11-5	11-7-6	15-9-0	16-0-5	16-4-2	H	7-3-0	10-3-0	11-11-4	13-1-2	14-0-0	14-7-6	15-1-3
M	4-8-4	8-6-1	12-2-0	14-8-7	15-4-0	16-3-0	M	5-2-1	7-4-4	8-11-0	10-1-3	11-1-4	12-0-4	12-10-0
O	5-0-4	8-10-0	12-5-4	13-3-2	14-9-4	16-1-4	O	3-11-4	5-7-6	6-11-1	8-0-3	9-0-5	10-0-4	11-1-1
Q	5-5-5	9-2-1	12-9-4	11-10-0	13-4-4	15-10-4	Q	2-6-3	3-10-2	4-10-0	5-8-4	6-7-5	7-7-4	8-8-2
S	5-10-6	9-6-6	13-2-0	9-10-4	12-7-4	15-5-4	S	1-3-0	2-2-4	2-10-4	3-5-5	4-1-5	4-11-1	5-10-5
U	6-4-7	10-0-1	13-7-4	7-0-0	10-6-0	14-8-6	U	0-4-4	0-9-0	1-1-6	1-6-4	1-11-0	2-4-2	3-0-0
W	7-0-0	10-6-2	13-10-4	3-4-4	6-8-4	12-3-3	W					0-3-2	0-5-4	0-9-1
X	7-4-0	10-9-3	14-0-6	1-8-6	4-5-0	10-4-2	X	Rake of stem from mull U	::	::	::	::	::	::
stem	7-10-0½	11-8-1	15-1-0	Rake ins. stem 13-7-4	Rake of stem from mull T 17-3-5	Rake of stem from mull U 23-0-0	stem	0-3-0	2-3-2	3-5-6	4-7-4	5-7-5	6-8-2	7-9-1

Water Lines 2 feet apart. Cross Seam Square at Top Height. Timbering room 3 feet. Heel of Stern-post 4'-6" aft of Mould 30. Rakes 2'-0 on 7 W.L. rakes 5'-2¼ on Cross Seam. Sided 13" at heel, 15" at cross seam. Deadrise 6". Rise of stem on H=⅜", M=1½", O=4", S=6⅝", U=1'-0". Stem rakes at rail heights on centre line 8'-11½" Stem sided 13" at heel, 13" at 4.9 w.l., 12½" at 7 w.l., 10" at main height, 9" at top height, 8" at rail.

TABLE OF OFFSETS OF CLIPPER SHIP "SEA WITCH"

Registered tonnage, 170'-3"; 33'-11"; 19'-0"; 907 53/95 tons. Capacity for cargo, 1,100 tons

A SHIP WITH DOUBLE TOPSAILS

INDEX

A CATALOG OF SELECTED

DOVER BOOKS

IN ALL FIELDS OF INTEREST

A CATALOG OF SELECTED DOVER
BOOKS IN ALL FIELDS OF INTEREST

THE ART NOUVEAU STYLE, edited by Roberta Waddell. 579 rare photographs of works in jewelry, metalwork, glass, ceramics, textiles, architecture and furniture by 175 artists—Mucha, Seguy, Lalique, Tiffany, many others. 288pp. 8⅜ × 11¼.
23515-7 Pa. $9.95

AMERICAN COUNTRY HOUSES OF THE GILDED AGE (Sheldon's "Artistic Country-Seats"), A. Lewis. All of Sheldon's fascinating and historically important photographs and plans. New text by Arnold Lewis. Approx. 200 illustrations. 128pp. 9⅜ × 12¼.
24301-X Pa. $7.95

THE WAY WE LIVE NOW, Anthony Trollope. Trollope's late masterpiece, marks shift to bitter satire. Character Melmotte "his greatest villain." Reproduced from original edition with 40 illustrations. 416pp. 6⅛ × 9¼.
24360-5 Pa. $7.95

BENCHLEY LOST AND FOUND, Robert Benchley. Finest humor from early 30's, about pet peeves, child psychologists, post office and others. Mostly unavailable elsewhere. 73 illustrations by Peter Arno and others. 183pp. 5⅜ × 8½.
22410-4 Pa. $3.50

ISOMETRIC PERSPECTIVE DESIGNS AND HOW TO CREATE THEM, John Locke. Isometric perspective is the picture of an object adrift in imaginary space. 75 mindboggling designs. 52pp. 8¼ × 11.
24123-8 Pa. $2.75

PERSPECTIVE FOR ARTISTS, Rex Vicat Cole. Depth, perspective of sky and sea, shadows, much more, not usually covered. 391 diagrams, 81 reproductions of drawings and paintings. 279pp. 5⅜ × 8½.
22487-2 Pa. $4.00

MOVIE-STAR PORTRAITS OF THE FORTIES, edited by John Kobal. 163 glamor, studio photos of 106 stars of the 1940s: Rita Hayworth, Ava Gardner, Marlon Brando, Clark Gable, many more. 176pp. 8⅜ × 11¼.
23546-7 Pa. $6.95

STARS OF THE BROADWAY STAGE, 1940-1967, Fred Fehl. Marlon Brando, Uta Hagen, John Kerr, John Gielgud, Jessica Tandy in great shows—*South Pacific, Galileo, West Side Story*, more. 240 black-and-white photos. 144pp. 8⅜ × 11¼.
24398-2 Pa. $8.95

ILLUSTRATED DICTIONARY OF HISTORIC ARCHITECTURE, edited by Cyril M. Harris. Extraordinary compendium of clear, concise definitions for over 5000 important architectural terms complemented by over 2000 line drawings. 592pp. 7½ × 9⅝.
24444-X Pa. $14.95

THE EARLY WORK OF FRANK LLOYD WRIGHT, F.L. Wright. 207 rare photos of Oak Park period, first great buildings: Unity Temple, Dana house, Larkin factory. Complete photos of Wasmuth edition. New Introduction. 160pp. 8⅜ × 11¼.
24381-8 Pa. $7.95

LIVING MY LIFE, Emma Goldman. Candid, no holds barred account by foremost American anarchist: her own life, anarchist movement, famous contemporaries, ideas and their impact. 944pp. 5⅜ × 8½. 22543-7, 22544-5 Pa., Two-vol. set $13.00

UNDERSTANDING THERMODYNAMICS, H.C. Van Ness. Clear, lucid treatment of first and second laws of thermodynamics. Excellent supplement to basic textbook in undergraduate science or engineering class. 103pp. 5⅜ × 8.
63277-6 Pa. $5.50

SMOCKING: TECHNIQUE, PROJECTS, AND DESIGNS, Dianne Durand. Foremost smocking designer provides complete instructions on how to smock. Over 10 projects, over 100 illustrations. 56pp. 8¼ × 11. 23788-5 Pa. $2.00

AUDUBON'S BIRDS IN COLOR FOR DECOUPAGE, edited by Eleanor H. Rawlings. 24 sheets, 37 most decorative birds, full color, on one side of paper. Instructions, including work under glass. 56pp. 8¼ × 11. 23492-4 Pa. $3.95

THE COMPLETE BOOK OF SILK SCREEN PRINTING PRODUCTION, J.I. Biegeleisen. For commercial user, teacher in advanced classes, serious hobbyist. Most modern techniques, materials, equipment for optimal results. 124 illustrations. 253pp. 5⅜ × 8½. 21100-2 Pa. $4.50

A TREASURY OF ART NOUVEAU DESIGN AND ORNAMENT, edited by Carol Belanger Grafton. 577 designs for the practicing artist. Full-page, spots, borders, bookplates by Klimt, Bradley, others. 144pp. 8⅜ × 11¼. 24001-0 Pa. $5.95

ART NOUVEAU TYPOGRAPHIC ORNAMENTS, Dan X. Solo. Over 800 Art Nouveau florals, swirls, women, animals, borders, scrolls, wreaths, spots and dingbats, copyright-free. 100pp. 8⅛ × 11. 24366-4 Pa. $4.00

HAND SHADOWS TO BE THROWN UPON THE WALL, Henry Bursill. Wonderful Victorian novelty tells how to make flying birds, dog, goose, deer, and 14 others, each explained by a full-page illustration. 32pp. 6½ × 9¼. 21779-5 Pa. $1.50

AUDUBON'S BIRDS OF AMERICA COLORING BOOK, John James Audubon. Rendered for coloring by Paul Kennedy. 46 of Audubon's noted illustrations: red-winged black-bird, cardinal, etc. Original plates reproduced in full-color on the covers. Captions. 48pp. 8¼ × 11. 23049-X Pa. $2.25

SILK SCREEN TECHNIQUES, J.I. Biegeleisen, M.A. Cohn. Clear, practical, modern, economical. Minimal equipment (self-built), materials, easy methods. For amateur, hobbyist, 1st book. 141 illustrations. 185pp. 6⅛ × 9¼. 20433-2 Pa. $3.95

101 PATCHWORK PATTERNS, Ruby S. McKim. 101 beautiful, immediately useable patterns, full-size, modern and traditional. Also general information, estimating, quilt lore. 140 illustrations. 124pp. 7⅞ × 10¾. 20773-0 Pa. $3.50

READY-TO-USE FLORAL DESIGNS, Ed Sibbett, Jr. Over 100 floral designs (most in three sizes) of popular individual blossoms as well as bouquets, sprays, garlands. 64pp. 8¼ × 11. 23976-4 Pa. $2.95

AMERICAN WILD FLOWERS COLORING BOOK, Paul Kennedy. Planned coverage of 46 most important wildflowers, from Rickett's collection; instructive as well as entertaining. Color versions on covers. Captions. 48pp. 8¼ × 11. 20095-7 Pa. $2.50

CARVING DUCK DECOYS, Harry V. Shourds and Anthony Hillman. Detailed instructions and full-size templates for constructing 16 beautiful, marvelously practical decoys according to time-honored South Jersey method. 70pp. 9¼ × 12¼. 24083-5 Pa. $4.95

TRADITIONAL PATCHWORK PATTERNS, Carol Belanger Grafton. Cardboard cut-out pieces for use as templates to make 12 quilts: Buttercup, Ribbon Border, Tree of Paradise, nine more. Full instructions. 57pp. 8¼ × 11. 23015-5 Pa. $3.50

25 KITES THAT FLY, Leslie Hunt. Full, easy-to-follow instructions for kites made from inexpensive materials. Many novelties. 70 illustrations. 110pp. 5⅜ × 8½.
22550-X Pa. $2.25

PIANO TUNING, J. Cree Fischer. Clearest, best book for beginner, amateur. Simple repairs, raising dropped notes, tuning by easy method of flattened fifths. No previous skills needed. 4 illustrations. 201pp. 5⅜ × 8½.
23267-0 Pa. $3.50

EARLY AMERICAN IRON-ON TRANSFER PATTERNS, edited by Rita Weiss. 75 designs, borders, alphabets, from traditional American sources. 48pp. 8¼ × 11.
23162-3 Pa. $1.95

CROCHETING EDGINGS, edited by Rita Weiss. Over 100 of the best designs for these lovely trims for a host of household items. Complete instructions, illustrations. 48pp. 8¼ × 11.
24031-2 Pa. $2.25

FINGER PLAYS FOR NURSERY AND KINDERGARTEN, Emilie Poulsson. 18 finger plays with music (voice and piano); entertaining, instructive. Counting, nature lore, etc. Victorian classic. 53 illustrations. 80pp. 6½ × 9¼. 22588-7 Pa. $1.95

BOSTON THEN AND NOW, Peter Vanderwarker. Here in 59 side-by-side views are photographic documentations of the city's past and present. 119 photographs. Full captions. 122pp. 8¼ × 11.
24312-5 Pa. $6.95

CROCHETING BEDSPREADS, edited by Rita Weiss. 22 patterns, originally published in three instruction books 1939-41. 39 photos, 8 charts. Instructions. 48pp. 8¼ × 11.
23610-2 Pa. $2.00

HAWTHORNE ON PAINTING, Charles W. Hawthorne. Collected from notes taken by students at famous Cape Cod School; hundreds of direct, personal *apercus*, ideas, suggestions. 91pp. 5⅜ × 8½.
20653-X Pa. $2.50

THERMODYNAMICS, Enrico Fermi. A classic of modern science. Clear, organized treatment of systems, first and second laws, entropy, thermodynamic potentials, etc. Calculus required. 160pp. 5⅜ × 8½.
60361-X Pa. $4.00

TEN BOOKS ON ARCHITECTURE, Vitruvius. The most important book ever written on architecture. Early Roman aesthetics, technology, classical orders, site selection, all other aspects. Morgan translation. 331pp. 5⅜ × 8½. 20645-9 Pa. $5.50

THE CORNELL BREAD BOOK, Clive M. McCay and Jeanette B. McCay. Famed high-protein recipe incorporated into breads, rolls, buns, coffee cakes, pizza, pie crusts, more. Nearly 50 illustrations. 48pp. 8¼ × 11.
23995-0 Pa. $2.00

THE CRAFTSMAN'S HANDBOOK, Cennino Cennini. 15th-century handbook, school of Giotto, explains applying gold, silver leaf; gesso; fresco painting, grinding pigments, etc. 142pp. 6⅛ × 9¼.
20054-X Pa. $3.50

FRANK LLOYD WRIGHT'S FALLINGWATER, Donald Hoffmann. Full story of Wright's masterwork at Bear Run, Pa. 100 photographs of site, construction, and details of completed structure. 112pp. 9¼ × 10.
23671-4 Pa. $6.95

OVAL STAINED GLASS PATTERN BOOK, C. Eaton. 60 new designs framed in shape of an oval. Greater complexity, challenge with sinuous cats, birds, mandalas framed in antique shape. 64pp. 8¼ × 11.
24519-5 Pa. $3.50

CHILDREN'S BOOKPLATES AND LABELS, Ed Sibbett, Jr. 6 each of 12 types based on *Wizard of Oz, Alice,* nursery rhymes, fairy tales. Perforated; full color. 24pp. 8¼ × 11. 23538-6 Pa. $3.50

READY-TO-USE VICTORIAN COLOR STICKERS: 96 Pressure-Sensitive Seals, Carol Belanger Grafton. Drawn from authentic period sources. Motifs include heads of men, women, children, plus florals, animals, birds, more. Will adhere to any clean surface. 8pp. 8½ × 11. 24551-9 Pa. $2.95

CUT AND FOLD PAPER SPACESHIPS THAT FLY, Michael Grater. 16 colorful, easy-to-build spaceships that really fly. Star Shuttle, Lunar Freighter, Star Probe, 13 others. 32pp. 8¼ × 11. 23978-0 Pa. $2.50

CUT AND ASSEMBLE PAPER AIRPLANES THAT FLY, Arthur Baker. 8 aerodynamically sound, ready-to-build paper airplanes, designed with latest techniques. Fly *Pegasus, Daedalus, Songbird,* 5 other aircraft. Instructions. 32pp. 9¼ × 11¼. 24302-8 Pa. $3.95

SIDELIGHTS ON RELATIVITY, Albert Einstein. Two lectures delivered in 1920-21: *Ether and Relativity* and *Geometry and Experience.* Elegant ideas in non-mathematical form. 56pp. 5⅜ × 8½. 24511-X Pa. $2.25

FADS AND FALLACIES IN THE NAME OF SCIENCE, Martin Gardner. Fair, witty appraisal of cranks and quacks of science: Velikovsky, orgone energy, Bridey Murphy, medical fads, etc. 373pp. 5⅜ × 8½. 20394-8 Pa. $5.95

VACATION HOMES AND CABINS, U.S. Dept. of Agriculture. Complete plans for 16 cabins, vacation homes and other shelters. 105pp. 9 × 12. 23631-5 Pa. $4.95

HOW TO BUILD A WOOD-FRAME HOUSE, L.O. Anderson. Placement, foundations, framing, sheathing, roof, insulation, plaster, finishing—almost everything else. 179 illustrations. 223pp. 7⅞ × 10¾. 22954-8 Pa. $5.50

THE MYSTERY OF A HANSOM CAB, Fergus W. Hume. Bizarre murder in a hansom cab leads to engrossing investigation. Memorable characters, rich atmosphere. 19th-century bestseller, still enjoyable, exciting. 256pp. 5⅜ × 8. 21956-9 Pa. $4.00

MANUAL OF TRADITIONAL WOOD CARVING, edited by Paul N. Hasluck. Possibly the best book in English on the craft of wood carving. Practical instructions, along with 1,146 working drawings and photographic illustrations. 576pp. 6½ × 9¼. 23489-4 Pa. $8.95

WHITTLING AND WOODCARVING, E.J Tangerman. Best book on market; clear, full. If you can cut a potato, you can carve toys, puzzles, chains, etc. Over 464 illustrations. 293pp. 5⅜ × 8½. 20965-2 Pa. $4.95

AMERICAN TRADEMARK DESIGNS, Barbara Baer Capitman. 732 marks, logos and corporate-identity symbols. Categories include entertainment, heavy industry, food and beverage. All black-and-white in standard forms. 160pp. 8⅛ × 11. 23259-X Pa. $6.95

DECORATIVE FRAMES AND BORDERS, edited by Edmund V. Gillon, Jr. Largest collection of borders and frames ever compiled for use of artists and designers. Renaissance, neo-Greek, Art Nouveau, Art Deco, to mention only a few styles. 396 illustrations. 192pp. 8⅜ × 11¼. 22928-9 Pa. $6.00

CATALOG OF DOVER BOOKS

THE MURDER BOOK OF J.G. REEDER, Edgar Wallace. Eight suspenseful stories by bestselling mystery writer of 20s and 30s. Features the donnish Mr. J.G. Reeder of Public Prosecutor's Office. 128pp. 5⅜ × 8½. (Available in U.S. only)
24374-5 Pa. $3.50

ANNE ORR'S CHARTED DESIGNS, Anne Orr. Best designs by premier needlework designer, all on charts: flowers, borders, birds, children, alphabets, etc. Over 100 charts, 10 in color. Total of 40pp. 8¼ × 11.
23704-4 Pa. $2.50

BASIC CONSTRUCTION TECHNIQUES FOR HOUSES AND SMALL BUILDINGS SIMPLY EXPLAINED, U.S. Bureau of Naval Personnel. Grading, masonry, woodworking, floor and wall framing, roof framing, plastering, tile setting, much more. Over 675 illustrations. 568pp. 6½ × 9¼.
20242-9 Pa. $8.95

MATISSE LINE DRAWINGS AND PRINTS, Henri Matisse. Representative collection of female nudes, faces, still lifes, experimental works, etc., from 1898 to 1948. 50 illustrations. 48pp. 8⅜ × 11¼.
23877-6 Pa. $2.50

HOW TO PLAY THE CHESS OPENINGS, Eugene Znosko-Borovsky. Clear, profound examinations of just what each opening is intended to do and how opponent can counter. Many sample games. 147pp. 5⅜ × 8½.
22795-2 Pa. $2.95

DUPLICATE BRIDGE, Alfred Sheinwold. Clear, thorough, easily followed account: rules, etiquette, scoring, strategy, bidding; Goren's point-count system, Blackwood and Gerber conventions, etc. 158pp. 5⅜ × 8½.
22741-3 Pa. $3.00

SARGENT PORTRAIT DRAWINGS, J.S. Sargent. Collection of 42 portraits reveals technical skill and intuitive eye of noted American portrait painter, John Singer Sargent. 48pp. 8¼ × 11⅛.
24524-1 Pa. $2.95

ENTERTAINING SCIENCE EXPERIMENTS WITH EVERYDAY OBJECTS, Martin Gardner. Over 100 experiments for youngsters. Will amuse, astonish, teach, and entertain. Over 100 illustrations. 127pp. 5⅜ × 8½.
24201-3 Pa. $2.50

TEDDY BEAR PAPER DOLLS IN FULL COLOR: A Family of Four Bears and Their Costumes, Crystal Collins. A family of four Teddy Bear paper dolls and nearly 60 cut-out costumes. Full color, printed one side only. 32pp. 9¼ × 12¼.
24550-0 Pa. $3.50

NEW CALLIGRAPHIC ORNAMENTS AND FLOURISHES, Arthur Baker. Unusual, multi-useable material: arrows, pointing hands, brackets and frames, ovals, swirls, birds, etc. Nearly 700 illustrations. 80pp. 8⅜ × 11¼.
24095-9 Pa. $3.75

DINOSAUR DIORAMAS TO CUT & ASSEMBLE, M. Kalmenoff. Two complete three-dimensional scenes in full color, with 31 cut-out animals and plants. Excellent educational toy for youngsters. Instructions; 2 assembly diagrams. 32pp. 9¼ × 12¼.
24541-1 Pa. $4.50

SILHOUETTES: A PICTORIAL ARCHIVE OF VARIED ILLUSTRATIONS, edited by Carol Belanger Grafton. Over 600 silhouettes from the 18th to 20th centuries. Profiles and full figures of men, women, children, birds, animals, groups and scenes, nature, ships, an alphabet. 144pp. 8⅜ × 11¼.
23781-8 Pa. $4.95

SURREAL STICKERS AND UNREAL STAMPS, William Rowe. 224 haunting, hilarious stamps on gummed, perforated stock, with images of elephants, geisha girls, George Washington, etc. 16pp. one side. 8¼ × 11.   24371-0 Pa. $3.50

GOURMET KITCHEN LABELS, Ed Sibbett, Jr. 112 full-color labels (4 copies each of 28 designs). Fruit, bread, other culinary motifs. Gummed and perforated. 16pp. 8¼ × 11.   24087-8 Pa. $2.95

PATTERNS AND INSTRUCTIONS FOR CARVING AUTHENTIC BIRDS, H.D. Green. Detailed instructions, 27 diagrams, 85 photographs for carving 15 species of birds so life-like, they'll seem ready to fly! 8¼ × 11.   24222-6 Pa. $2.75

FLATLAND, E.A. Abbott. Science-fiction classic explores life of 2-D being in 3-D world. 16 illustrations. 103pp. 5⅜ × 8.   20001-9 Pa. $2.00

DRIED FLOWERS, Sarah Whitlock and Martha Rankin. Concise, clear, practical guide to dehydration, glycerinizing, pressing plant material, and more. Covers use of silica gel. 12 drawings. 32pp. 5⅜ × 8½.   21802-3 Pa. $1.00

EASY-TO-MAKE CANDLES, Gary V. Guy. Learn how easy it is to make all kinds of decorative candles. Step-by-step instructions. 82 illustrations. 48pp. 8¼ × 11.
23881-4 Pa. $2.50

SUPER STICKERS FOR KIDS, Carolyn Bracken. 128 gummed and perforated full-color stickers: GIRL WANTED, KEEP OUT, BORED OF EDUCATION, X-RATED, COMBAT ZONE, many others. 16pp. 8¼ × 11.   24092-4 Pa. $2.50

CUT AND COLOR PAPER MASKS, Michael Grater. Clowns, animals, funny faces...simply color them in, cut them out, and put them together, and you have 9 paper masks to play with and enjoy. 32pp. 8¼ × 11.   23171-2 Pa. $2.25

A CHRISTMAS CAROL: THE ORIGINAL MANUSCRIPT, Charles Dickens. Clear facsimile of Dickens manuscript, on facing pages with final printed text. 8 illustrations by John Leech, 4 in color on covers. 144pp. 8⅜ × 11¼.
20980-6 Pa. $5.95

CARVING SHOREBIRDS, Harry V. Shourds & Anthony Hillman. 16 full-size patterns (all double-page spreads) for 19 North American shorebirds with step-by-step instructions. 72pp. 9¼ × 12¼.   24287-0 Pa. $4.95

THE GENTLE ART OF MATHEMATICS, Dan Pedoe. Mathematical games, probability, the question of infinity, topology, how the laws of algebra work, problems of irrational numbers, and more. 42 figures. 143pp. 5⅜ × 8½. (EBE)
22949-1 Pa. $3.50

READY-TO-USE DOLLHOUSE WALLPAPER, Katzenbach & Warren, Inc. Stripe, 2 floral stripes, 2 allover florals, polka dot; all in full color. 4 sheets (350 sq. in.) of each, enough for average room. 48pp. 8¼ × 11.   23495-9 Pa. $2.95

MINIATURE IRON-ON TRANSFER PATTERNS FOR DOLLHOUSES, DOLLS, AND SMALL PROJECTS, Rita Weiss and Frank Fontana. Over 100 miniature patterns: rugs, bedspreads, quilts, chair seats, etc. In standard dollhouse size. 48pp. 8¼ × 11.   23741-9 Pa. $1.95

THE DINOSAUR COLORING BOOK, Anthony Rao. 45 renderings of dinosaurs, fossil birds, turtles, other creatures of Mesozoic Era. Scientifically accurate. Captions. 48pp. 8¼ × 11.   24022-3 Pa. $2.50

THE BOOK OF WOOD CARVING, Charles Marshall Sayers. Still finest book for beginning student. Fundamentals, technique; gives 34 designs, over 34 projects for panels, bookends, mirrors, etc. 33 photos. 118pp. 7¾ × 10⅝. 23654-4 Pa. $3.95

CARVING COUNTRY CHARACTERS, Bill Higginbotham. Expert advice for beginning, advanced carvers on materials, techniques for creating 18 projects— mirthful panorama of American characters. 105 illustrations. 80pp. 8⅜ × 11.
24135-1 Pa. $2.50

300 ART NOUVEAU DESIGNS AND MOTIFS IN FULL COLOR, C.B. Grafton. 44 full-page plates display swirling lines and muted colors typical of Art Nouveau. Borders, frames, panels, cartouches, dingbats, etc. 48pp. 9⅜ × 12¼.
24354-0 Pa. $6.95

SELF-WORKING CARD TRICKS, Karl Fulves. Editor of *Pallbearer* offers 72 tricks that work automatically through nature of card deck. No sleight of hand needed. Often spectacular. 42 illustrations. 113pp. 5⅜ × 8½. 23334-0 Pa. $3.50

CUT AND ASSEMBLE A WESTERN FRONTIER TOWN, Edmund V. Gillon, Jr. Ten authentic full-color buildings on heavy cardboard stock in H-O scale. Sheriff's Office and Jail, Saloon, Wells Fargo, Opera House, others. 48pp. 9¼ × 12¼.
23736-2 Pa. $3.95

CUT AND ASSEMBLE AN EARLY NEW ENGLAND VILLAGE, Edmund V. Gillon, Jr. Printed in full color on heavy cardboard stock. 12 authentic buildings in H-O scale: Adams home in Quincy, Mass., Oliver Wight house in Sturbridge, smithy, store, church, others. 48pp. 9¼ × 12¼. 23536-X Pa. $4.95

THE TALE OF TWO BAD MICE, Beatrix Potter. Tom Thumb and Hunca Munca squeeze out of their hole and go exploring. 27 full-color Potter illustrations. 59pp. 4¼ × 5½. (Available in U.S. only) 23065-1 Pa. $1.75

CARVING FIGURE CARICATURES IN THE OZARK STYLE, Harold L. Enlow. Instructions and illustrations for ten delightful projects, plus general carving instructions. 22 drawings and 47 photographs altogether. 39pp. 8⅜ × 11.
23151-8 Pa. $2.50

A TREASURY OF FLOWER DESIGNS FOR ARTISTS, EMBROIDERERS AND CRAFTSMEN, Susan Gaber. 100 garden favorites lushly rendered by artist for artists, craftsmen, needleworkers. Many form frames, borders. 80pp. 8¼ × 11.
24096-7 Pa. $3.50

CUT & ASSEMBLE A TOY THEATER/THE NUTCRACKER BALLET, Tom Tierney. Model of a complete, full-color production of Tchaikovsky's classic. 6 backdrops, dozens of characters, familiar dance sequences. 32pp. 9⅜ × 12¼.
24194-7 Pa. $4.50

ANIMALS: 1,419 COPYRIGHT-FREE ILLUSTRATIONS OF MAMMALS, BIRDS, FISH, INSECTS, ETC., edited by Jim Harter. Clear wood engravings present, in extremely lifelike poses, over 1,000 species of animals. 284pp. 9 × 12.
23766-4 Pa. $9.95

MORE HAND SHADOWS, Henry Bursill. For those at their 'finger ends," 16 more effects—Shakespeare, a hare, a squirrel, Mr. Punch, and twelve more—each explained by a full-page illustration. Considerable period charm. 30pp. 6½ × 9¼.
21384-6 Pa. $1.95

JAPANESE DESIGN MOTIFS, Matsuya Co. Mon, or heraldic designs. Over 4000 typical, beautiful designs: birds, animals, flowers, swords, fans, geometrics; all beautifully stylized. 213pp. 11⅜ × 8¼. 22874-6 Pa. $7.95

THE TALE OF BENJAMIN BUNNY, Beatrix Potter. Peter Rabbit's cousin coaxes him back into Mr. McGregor's garden for a whole new set of adventures. All 27 full-color illustrations. 59pp. 4¼ × 5½. (Available in U.S. only) 21102-9 Pa. $1.75

THE TALE OF PETER RABBIT AND OTHER FAVORITE STORIES BOXED SET, Beatrix Potter. Seven of Beatrix Potter's best-loved tales including Peter Rabbit in a specially designed, durable boxed set. 4¼ × 5½. Total of 447pp. 158 color illustrations. (Available in U.S. only) 23903-9 Pa. $10.80

PRACTICAL MENTAL MAGIC, Theodore Annemann. Nearly 200 astonishing feats of mental magic revealed in step-by-step detail. Complete advice on staging, patter, etc. Illustrated. 320pp. 5⅜ × 8½. 24426-1 Pa. $5.95

CELEBRATED CASES OF JUDGE DEE (DEE GOONG AN), translated by Robert Van Gulik. Authentic 18th-century Chinese detective novel; Dee and associates solve three interlocked cases. Led to van Gulik's own stories with same characters. Extensive introduction. 9 illustrations. 237pp. 5⅜ × 8½. 23337-5 Pa. $4.50

CUT & FOLD EXTRATERRESTRIAL INVADERS THAT FLY, M. Grater. Stage your own lilliputian space battles.By following the step-by-step instructions and explanatory diagrams you can launch 22 full-color fliers into space. 36pp. 8¼ × 11. 24478-4 Pa. $2.95

CUT & ASSEMBLE VICTORIAN HOUSES, Edmund V. Gillon, Jr. Printed in full color on heavy cardboard stock, 4 authentic Victorian houses in H-O scale: Italian-style Villa, Octagon, Second Empire, Stick Style. 48pp. 9¼ × 12¼. 23849-0 Pa. $3.95

BEST SCIENCE FICTION STORIES OF H.G. WELLS, H.G. Wells. Full novel *The Invisible Man,* plus 17 short stories: "The Crystal Egg," "Aepyornis Island," "The Strange Orchid," etc. 303pp. 5⅜ × 8½. (Available in U.S. only) 21531-8 Pa. $4.95

TRADEMARK DESIGNS OF THE WORLD, Yusaku Kamekura. A lavish collection of nearly 700 trademarks, the work of Wright, Loewy, Klee, Binder, hundreds of others. 160pp. 8¾ × 8. (Available in U.S. only) 24191-2 Pa. $5.95

THE ARTIST'S AND CRAFTSMAN'S GUIDE TO REDUCING, ENLARGING AND TRANSFERRING DESIGNS, Rita Weiss. Discover, reduce, enlarge, transfer designs from any objects to any craft project. 12pp. plus 16 sheets special graph paper. 8¼ × 11. 24142-4 Pa. $3.50

TREASURY OF JAPANESE DESIGNS AND MOTIFS FOR ARTISTS AND CRAFTSMEN, edited by Carol Belanger Grafton. Indispensable collection of 360 traditional Japanese designs and motifs redrawn in clean, crisp black-and-white, copyright-free illustrations. 96pp. 8¼ × 11. 24435-0 Pa. $3.95

CHANCERY CURSIVE STROKE BY STROKE, Arthur Baker. Instructions and illustrations for each stroke of each letter (upper and lower case) and numerals. 54 full-page plates. 64pp. 8¼ × 11. 24278-1 Pa. $2.50

THE ENJOYMENT AND USE OF COLOR, Walter Sargent. Color relationships, values, intensities; complementary colors, illumination, similar topics. Color in nature and art. 7 color plates, 29 illustrations. 274pp. 5⅜ × 8½. 20944-X Pa. $4.95

SCULPTURE PRINCIPLES AND PRACTICE, Louis Slobodkin. Step-by-step approach to clay, plaster, metals, stone; classical and modern. 253 drawings, photos. 255pp. 8⅛ × 11. 22960-2 Pa. $7.50

VICTORIAN FASHION PAPER DOLLS FROM HARPER'S BAZAR, 1867-1898, Theodore Menten. Four female dolls with 28 elegant high fashion costumes, printed in full color. 32pp. 9¼ × 12¼. 23453-3 Pa. $3.50

FLOPSY, MOPSY AND COTTONTAIL: A Little Book of Paper Dolls in Full Color, Susan LaBelle. Three dolls and 21 costumes (7 for each doll) show Peter Rabbit's siblings dressed for holidays, gardening, hiking, etc. Charming borders, captions. 48pp. 4¼ × 5½. 24376-1 Pa. $2.25

NATIONAL LEAGUE BASEBALL CARD CLASSICS, Bert Randolph Sugar. 83 big-leaguers from 1909-69 on facsimile cards. Hubbell, Dean, Spahn, Brock plus advertising, info, no duplications. Perforated, detachable. 16pp. 8¼ × 11. 24308-7 Pa. $2.95

THE LOGICAL APPROACH TO CHESS, Dr. Max Euwe, et al. First-rate text of comprehensive strategy, tactics, theory for the amateur. No gambits to memorize, just a clear, logical approach. 224pp. 5⅜ × 8½. 24353-2 Pa. $4.50

MAGICK IN THEORY AND PRACTICE, Aleister Crowley. The summation of the thought and practice of the century's most famous necromancer, long hard to find. Crowley's best book. 436pp. 5⅜ × 8½. (Available in U.S. only) 23295-6 Pa. $6.50

THE HAUNTED HOTEL, Wilkie Collins. Collins' last great tale; doom and destiny in a Venetian palace. Praised by T.S. Eliot. 127pp. 5⅜ × 8½. 24333-8 Pa. $3.00

ART DECO DISPLAY ALPHABETS, Dan X. Solo. Wide variety of bold yet elegant lettering in handsome Art Deco styles. 100 complete fonts, with numerals, punctuation, more. 104pp. 8⅛ × 11. 24372-9 Pa. $4.50

CALLIGRAPHIC ALPHABETS, Arthur Baker. Nearly 150 complete alphabets by outstanding contemporary. Stimulating ideas; useful source for unique effects. 154 plates. 157pp. 8⅜ × 11¼. 21045-6 Pa. $5.95

ARTHUR BAKER'S HISTORIC CALLIGRAPHIC ALPHABETS, Arthur Baker. From monumental capitals of first-century Rome to humanistic cursive of 16th century, 33 alphabets in fresh interpretations. 88 plates. 96pp. 9 × 12. 24054-1 Pa. $4.50

LETTIE LANE PAPER DOLLS, Sheila Young. Genteel turn-of-the-century family very popular then and now. 24 paper dolls. 16 plates in full color. 32pp. 9¼ × 12¼. 24089-4 Pa. $3.50

TWENTY-FOUR ART NOUVEAU POSTCARDS IN FULL COLOR FROM CLASSIC POSTERS, Hayward and Blanche Cirker. Ready-to-mail postcards reproduced from rare set of poster art. Works by Toulouse-Lautrec, Parrish, Steinlen, Mucha, Cheret, others. 12pp. 8¼× 11. 24389-3 Pa. $2.95

READY-TO-USE ART NOUVEAU BOOKMARKS IN FULL COLOR, Carol Belanger Grafton. 30 elegant bookmarks featuring graceful, flowing lines, foliate motifs, sensuous women characteristic of Art Nouveau. Perforated for easy detaching. 16pp. 8¼ × 11. 24305-2 Pa. $2.95

FRUIT KEY AND TWIG KEY TO TREES AND SHRUBS, William M. Harlow. Fruit key covers 120 deciduous and evergreen species; twig key covers 160 deciduous species. Easily used. Over 300 photographs. 126pp. 5⅜ × 8½. 20511-8 Pa. $2.25

LEONARDO DRAWINGS, Leonardo da Vinci. Plants, landscapes, human face and figure, etc., plus studies for Sforza monument, *Last Supper*, more. 60 illustrations. 64pp. 8¼ × 11⅛. 23951-9 Pa. $2.75

CLASSIC BASEBALL CARDS, edited by Bert R. Sugar. 98 classic cards on heavy stock, full color, perforated for detaching. Ruth, Cobb, Durocher, DiMaggio, H. Wagner, 99 others. Rare originals cost hundreds. 16pp. 8¼ × 11. 23498-3 Pa. $3.25

TREES OF THE EASTERN AND CENTRAL UNITED STATES AND CANADA, William M. Harlow. Best one-volume guide to 140 trees. Full descriptions, woodlore, range, etc. Over 600 illustrations. Handy size. 288pp. 4½ × 6⅜. 20395-6 Pa. $3.95

JUDY GARLAND PAPER DOLLS IN FULL COLOR, Tom Tierney. 3 Judy Garland paper dolls (teenager, grown-up, and mature woman) and 30 gorgeous costumes highlighting memorable career. Captions. 32pp. 9¼ × 12¼. 24404-0 Pa. $3.50

GREAT FASHION DESIGNS OF THE BELLE EPOQUE PAPER DOLLS IN FULL COLOR, Tom Tierney. Two dolls and 30 costumes meticulously rendered. Haute couture by Worth, Lanvin, Paquin, other greats late Victorian to WWI. 32pp. 9¼ × 12¼. 24425-3 Pa. $3.50

FASHION PAPER DOLLS FROM GODEY'S LADY'S BOOK, 1840-1854, Susan Johnston. In full color: 7 female fashion dolls with 50 costumes. Little girl's, bridal, riding, bathing, wedding, evening, everyday, etc. 32pp. 9¼ × 12¼. 23511-4 Pa. $3.95

THE BOOK OF THE SACRED MAGIC OF ABRAMELIN THE MAGE, translated by S. MacGregor Mathers. Medieval manuscript of ceremonial magic. Basic document in Aleister Crowley, Golden Dawn groups. 268pp. 5⅜ × 8½. 23211-5 Pa. $5.00

PETER RABBIT POSTCARDS IN FULL COLOR: 24 Ready-to-Mail Cards, Susan Whited LaBelle. Bunnies ice-skating, coloring Easter eggs, making valentines, many other charming scenes. 24 perforated full-color postcards, each measuring 4¼ × 6, on coated stock. 12pp. 9 × 12. 24617-5 Pa. $2.95

CELTIC HAND STROKE BY STROKE, A. Baker. Complete guide creating each letter of the alphabet in distinctive Celtic manner. Covers hand position, strokes, pens, inks, paper, more. Illustrated. 48pp. 8¼ × 11. 24336-2 Pa. $2.50

KEYBOARD WORKS FOR SOLO INSTRUMENTS, G.F. Handel. 35 neglected works from Handel's vast oeuvre, originally jotted down as improvisations. Includes Eight Great Suites, others. New sequence. 174pp. 9⅜ × 12¼.

24338-9 Pa. $7.50

AMERICAN LEAGUE BASEBALL CARD CLASSICS, Bert Randolph Sugar. 82 stars from 1900s to 60s on facsimile cards. Ruth, Cobb, Mantle, Williams, plus advertising, info, no duplications. Perforated, detachable. 16pp. 8¼ × 11.

24286-2 Pa. $2.95

A TREASURY OF CHARTED DESIGNS FOR NEEDLEWORKERS, Georgia Gorham and Jeanne Warth. 141 charted designs: owl, cat with yarn, tulips, piano, spinning wheel, covered bridge, Victorian house and many others. 48pp. 8¼ × 11.

23558-0 Pa. $1.95

DANISH FLORAL CHARTED DESIGNS, Gerda Bengtsson. Exquisite collection of over 40 different florals: anemone, Iceland poppy, wild fruit, pansies, many others. 45 illustrations. 48pp. 8¼ × 11.   23957-8 Pa. $1.75

OLD PHILADELPHIA IN EARLY PHOTOGRAPHS 1839-1914, Robert F. Looney. 215 photographs: panoramas, street scenes, landmarks, President-elect Lincoln's visit, 1876 Centennial Exposition, much more. 230pp. 8⅜ × 11¼.

23345-6 Pa. $9.95

PRELUDE TO MATHEMATICS, W.W. Sawyer. Noted mathematician's lively, stimulating account of non-Euclidean geometry, matrices, determinants, group theory, other topics. Emphasis on novel, striking aspects. 224pp. 5⅜ × 8½.

24401-6 Pa. $4.50

ADVENTURES WITH A MICROSCOPE, Richard Headstrom. 59 adventures with clothing fibers, protozoa, ferns and lichens, roots and leaves, much more. 142 illustrations. 232pp. 5⅜ × 8½.   23471-1 Pa. $3.95

IDENTIFYING ANIMAL TRACKS: MAMMALS, BIRDS, AND OTHER ANIMALS OF THE EASTERN UNITED STATES, Richard Headstrom. For hunters, naturalists, scouts, nature-lovers. Diagrams of tracks, tips on identification. 128pp. 5⅜ × 8.   24442-3 Pa. $3.50

VICTORIAN FASHIONS AND COSTUMES FROM HARPER'S BAZAR, 1867-1898, edited by Stella Blum. Day costumes, evening wear, sports clothes, shoes, hats, other accessories in over 1,000 detailed engravings. 320pp. 9⅜ × 12¼.

22990-4 Pa. $10.95

EVERYDAY FASHIONS OF THE TWENTIES AS PICTURED IN SEARS AND OTHER CATALOGS, edited by Stella Blum. Actual dress of the Roaring Twenties, with text by Stella Blum. Over 750 illustrations, captions. 156pp. 9 × 12.

24134-3 Pa. $8.50

HALL OF FAME BASEBALL CARDS, edited by Bert Randolph Sugar. Cy Young, Ted Williams, Lou Gehrig, and many other Hall of Fame greats on 92 full-color, detachable reprints of early baseball cards. No duplication of cards with *Classic Baseball Cards*. 16pp. 8¼ × 11.   23624-2 Pa. $3.50

THE ART OF HAND LETTERING, Helm Wotzkow. Course in hand lettering, Roman, Gothic, Italic, Block, Script. Tools, proportions, optical aspects, individual variation. Very quality conscious. Hundreds of specimens. 320pp. 5⅜ × 8½.

21797-3 Pa. $4.95

CATALOG OF DOVER BOOKS

HOW THE OTHER HALF LIVES, Jacob A. Riis. Journalistic record of filth, degradation, upward drive in New York immigrant slums, shops, around 1900. New edition includes 100 original Riis photos, monuments of early photography. 233pp. 10 × 7⅞. 22012-5 Pa. $7.95

CHINA AND ITS PEOPLE IN EARLY PHOTOGRAPHS, John Thomson. In 200 black-and-white photographs of exceptional quality photographic pioneer Thomson captures the mountains, dwellings, monuments and people of 19th-century China. 272pp. 9⅜ × 12¼. 24393-1 Pa. $12.95

GODEY COSTUME PLATES IN COLOR FOR DECOUPAGE AND FRAMING, edited by Eleanor Hasbrouk Rawlings. 24 full-color engravings depicting 19th-century Parisian haute couture. Printed on one side only. 56pp. 8¼ × 11. 23879-2 Pa. $3.95

ART NOUVEAU STAINED GLASS PATTERN BOOK, Ed Sibbett, Jr. 104 projects using well-known themes of Art Nouveau: swirling forms, florals, peacocks, and sensuous women. 60pp. 8¼ × 11. 23577-7 Pa. $3.50

QUICK AND EASY PATCHWORK ON THE SEWING MACHINE: Susan Aylsworth Murwin and Suzzy Payne. Instructions, diagrams show exactly how to machine sew 12 quilts. 48pp. of templates. 50 figures. 80pp. 8¼ × 11. 23770-2 Pa. $3.50

THE STANDARD BOOK OF QUILT MAKING AND COLLECTING, Marguerite Ickis. Full information, full-sized patterns for making 46 traditional quilts, also 150 other patterns. 483 illustrations. 273pp. 6⅞ × 9⅝. 20582-7 Pa. $5.95

LETTERING AND ALPHABETS, J. Albert Cavanagh. 85 complete alphabets lettered in various styles; instructions for spacing, roughs, brushwork. 121pp. 8¾ × 8. 20053-1 Pa. $3.95

LETTER FORMS: 110 COMPLETE ALPHABETS, Frederick Lambert. 110 sets of capital letters; 16 lower case alphabets; 70 sets of numbers and other symbols. 110pp. 8⅛ × 11. 22872-X Pa. $4.50

ORCHIDS AS HOUSE PLANTS, Rebecca Tyson Northen. Grow cattleyas and many other kinds of orchids—in a window, in a case, or under artificial light. 63 illustrations. 148pp. 5⅜ × 8½. 23261-1 Pa. $2.95

THE MUSHROOM HANDBOOK, Louis C.C. Krieger. Still the best popular handbook. Full descriptions of 259 species, extremely thorough text, poisons, folklore, etc. 32 color plates; 126 other illustrations. 560pp. 5⅜ × 8½. 21861-9 Pa. $8.50

THE DORÉ BIBLE ILLUSTRATIONS, Gustave Doré. All wonderful, detailed plates: Adam and Eve, Flood, Babylon, life of Jesus, etc. Brief King James text with each plate. 241 plates. 241pp. 9 × 12. 23004-X Pa. $8.95

THE BOOK OF KELLS: Selected Plates in Full Color, edited by Blanche Cirker. 32 full-page plates from greatest manuscript-icon of early Middle Ages. Fantastic, mysterious. Publisher's Note. Captions. 32pp. 9¾ × 12¼. 24345-1 Pa. $4.50

THE PERFECT WAGNERITE, George Bernard Shaw. Brilliant criticism of the Ring Cycle, with provocative interpretation of politics, economic theories behind the Ring. 136pp. 5⅜ × 8½. (Available in U.S. only) 21707-8 Pa. $3.00

THE RIME OF THE ANCIENT MARINER, Gustave Doré, S.T. Coleridge. Doré's finest work, 34 plates capture moods, subtleties of poem. Full text. 77pp. 9¼ × 12. 22305-1 Pa. $4.95

SONGS OF INNOCENCE, William Blake. The first and most popular of Blake's famous "Illuminated Books," in a facsimile edition reproducing all 31 brightly colored plates. Additional printed text of each poem. 64pp. 5¼ × 7. 22764-2 Pa. $3.50

AN INTRODUCTION TO INFORMATION THEORY, J.R. Pierce. Second (1980) edition of most impressive non-technical account available. Encoding, entropy, noisy channel, related areas, etc. 320pp. 5⅜ × 8½. 24061-4 Pa. $4.95

THE DIVINE PROPORTION: A STUDY IN MATHEMATICAL BEAUTY, H.E. Huntley. "Divine proportion" or "golden ratio" in poetry, Pascal's triangle, philosophy, psychology, music, mathematical figures, etc. Excellent bridge between science and art. 58 figures. 185pp. 5⅜ × 8½. 22254-3 Pa. $3.95

THE DOVER NEW YORK WALKING GUIDE: From the Battery to Wall Street, Mary J. Shapiro. Superb inexpensive guide to historic buildings and locales in lower Manhattan: Trinity Church, Bowling Green, more. Complete Text; maps. 36 illustrations. 48pp. 3⅞ × 9¼. 24225-0 Pa. $2.50

NEW YORK THEN AND NOW, Edward B. Watson, Edmund V. Gillon, Jr. 83 important Manhattan sites: on facing pages early photographs (1875-1925) and 1976 photos by Gillon. 172 illustrations. 171pp. 9¼ × 10. 23361-8 Pa. $7.95

HISTORIC COSTUME IN PICTURES, Braun & Schneider. Over 1450 costumed figures from dawn of civilization to end of 19th century. English captions. 125 plates. 256pp. 8⅜ × 11¼. 23150-X Pa. $7.50

VICTORIAN AND EDWARDIAN FASHION: A Photographic Survey, Alison Gernsheim. First fashion history completely illustrated by contemporary photographs. Full text plus 235 photos, 1840-1914, in which many celebrities appear. 240pp. 6½ × 9¼. 24205-6 Pa. $6.00

CHARTED CHRISTMAS DESIGNS FOR COUNTED CROSS-STITCH AND OTHER NEEDLECRAFTS, Lindberg Press. Charted designs for 45 beautiful needlecraft projects with many yuletide and wintertime motifs. 48pp. 8¼ × 11. 24356-7 Pa. $2.50

101 FOLK DESIGNS FOR COUNTED CROSS-STITCH AND OTHER NEEDLE-CRAFTS, Carter Houck. 101 authentic charted folk designs in a wide array of lovely representations with many suggestions for effective use. 48pp. 8¼ × 11. 24369-9 Pa. $2.25

FIVE ACRES AND INDEPENDENCE, Maurice G. Kains. Great back-to-the-land classic explains basics of self-sufficient farming. The one book to get. 95 illustrations. 397pp. 5⅜ × 8½. 20974-1 Pa. $4.95

A MODERN HERBAL, Margaret Grieve. Much the fullest, most exact, most useful compilation of herbal material. Gigantic alphabetical encyclopedia, from aconite to zedoary, gives botanical information, medical properties, folklore, economic uses, and much else. Indispensable to serious reader. 161 illustrations. 888pp. 6½ × 9¼. (Available in U.S. only) 22798-7, 22799-5 Pa., Two-vol. set $16.45

REASON IN ART, George Santayana. Renowned philosopher's provocative, seminal treatment of basis of art in instinct and experience. Volume Four of *The Life of Reason.* 230pp. 5⅜ × 8. 24358-3 Pa. $4.50

LANGUAGE, TRUTH AND LOGIC, Alfred J. Ayer. Famous, clear introduction to Vienna, Cambridge schools of Logical Positivism. Role of philosophy, elimination of metaphysics, nature of analysis, etc. 160pp. 5⅜ × 8½. (USCO)
20010-8 Pa. $2.75

BASIC ELECTRONICS, U.S. Bureau of Naval Personnel. Electron tubes, circuits, antennas, AM, FM, and CW transmission and receiving, etc. 560 illustrations. 567pp. 6½ × 9¼. 21076-6 Pa. $8.95

THE ART DECO STYLE, edited by Theodore Menten. Furniture, jewelry, metalwork, ceramics, fabrics, lighting fixtures, interior decors, exteriors, graphics from pure French sources. Over 400 photographs. 183pp. 8⅜ × 11¼.
22824-X Pa. $6.95

THE FOUR BOOKS OF ARCHITECTURE, Andrea Palladio. 16th-century classic covers classical architectural remains, Renaissance revivals, classical orders, etc. 1738 Ware English edition. 216 plates. 110pp. of text. 9½ × 12¾.
21308-0 Pa. $11.50

THE WIT AND HUMOR OF OSCAR WILDE, edited by Alvin Redman. More than 1000 ripostes, paradoxes, wisecracks: Work is the curse of the drinking classes, I can resist everything except temptations, etc. 258pp. 5⅜ × 8½. (USCO)
20602-5 Pa. $3.95

THE DEVIL'S DICTIONARY, Ambrose Bierce. Barbed, bitter, brilliant witticisms in the form of a dictionary. Best, most ferocious satire America has produced. 145pp. 5⅜ × 8½. 20487-1 Pa. $2.50

ERTÉ'S FASHION DESIGNS, Erté. 210 black-and-white inventions from *Harper's Bazar*, 1918-32, plus 8pp. full-color covers. Captions. 88pp. 9 × 12.
24203-X Pa. $6.50

ERTÉ GRAPHICS, Erté. Collection of striking color graphics: *Seasons, Alphabet, Numerals, Aces* and *Precious Stones.* 50 plates, including 4 on covers. 48pp. 9⅜ × 12¼. 23580-7 Pa. $6.95

PAPER FOLDING FOR BEGINNERS, William D. Murray and Francis J. Rigney. Clearest book for making origami sail boats, roosters, frogs that move legs, etc. 40 projects. More than 275 illustrations. 94pp. 5⅜ × 8½. 20713-7 Pa. $2.25

ORIGAMI FOR THE ENTHUSIAST, John Montroll. Fish, ostrich, peacock, squirrel, rhinoceros, Pegasus, 19 other intricate subjects. Instructions. Diagrams. 128pp. 9 × 12. 23799-0 Pa. $4.95

CROCHETING NOVELTY POT HOLDERS, edited by Linda Macho. 64 useful, whimsical pot holders feature kitchen themes, animals, flowers, other novelties. Surprisingly easy to crochet. Complete instructions. 48pp. 8¼ × 11.
24296-X Pa. $1.95

CROCHETING DOILIES, edited by Rita Weiss. Irish Crochet, Jewel, Star Wheel, Vanity Fair and more. Also luncheon and console sets, runners and centerpieces. 51 illustrations. 48pp. 8¼ × 11. 23424-X Pa. $2.50

CATALOG OF DOVER BOOKS

TOLL HOUSE TRIED AND TRUE RECIPES, Ruth Graves Wakefield. Popovers, veal and ham loaf, baked beans, much more from the famous Mass. restaurant. Nearly 700 recipes. 376pp. 5⅜ × 8½. 23560-2 Pa. $4.95

FAVORITE CHRISTMAS CAROLS, selected and arranged by Charles J.F. Cofone. Title, music, first verse and refrain of 34 traditional carols in handsome calligraphy; also subsequent verses and other information in type. 79pp. 8⅜ × 11. 20445-6 Pa. $3.50

CAMERA WORK: A PICTORIAL GUIDE, Alfred Stieglitz. All 559 illustrations from most important periodical in history of art photography. Reduced in size but still clear, in strict chronological order, with complete captions. 176pp. 8⅜ × 11¼. 23591-2 Pa. $6.95

FAVORITE SONGS OF THE NINETIES, edited by Robert Fremont. 88 favorites: "Ta-Ra-Ra-Boom-De-Aye," "The Band Played On," "Bird in a Gilded Cage," etc. 401pp. 9 × 12. 21536-9 Pa. $12.95

STRING FIGURES AND HOW TO MAKE THEM, Caroline F. Jayne. Fullest, clearest instructions on string figures from around world: Eskimo, Navajo, Lapp, Europe, more. Cat's cradle, moving spear, lightning, stars. 950 illustrations. 407pp. 5⅜ × 8½. 20152-X Pa. $5.95

LIFE IN ANCIENT EGYPT, Adolf Erman. Detailed older account, with much not in more recent books: domestic life, religion, magic, medicine, commerce, and whatever else needed for complete picture. Many illustrations. 597pp. 5⅜ × 8½. 22632-8 Pa. $7.95

ANCIENT EGYPT: ITS CULTURE AND HISTORY, J.E. Manchip White. From pre-dynastics through Ptolemies: scoiety, history, political structure, religion, daily life, literature, cultural heritage. 48 plates. 217pp. 5⅜ × 8½. (EBE) 22548-8 Pa. $4.95

KEPT IN THE DARK, Anthony Trollope. Unusual short novel about Victorian morality and abnormal psychology by the great English author. Probably the first American publication. Frontispiece by Sir John Millais. 92pp. 6½ × 9¼. 23609-9 Pa. $2.95

MAN AND WIFE, Wilkie Collins. Nineteenth-century master launches an attack on out-moded Scottish marital laws and Victorian cult of athleticism. Artfully plotted. 35 illustrations. 239pp. 6⅛ × 9¼. 24451-2 Pa. $5.95

RELATIVITY AND COMMON SENSE, Herman Bondi. Radically reoriented presentation of Einstein's Special Theory and one of most valuable popular accounts available. 60 illustrations. 177pp. 5⅜ × 8. (EUK) 24021-5 Pa. $3.95

THE EGYPTIAN BOOK OF THE DEAD, E.A. Wallis Budge. Complete reproduction of Ani's papyrus, finest ever found. Full hieroglyphic text, interlinear transliteration, word-for-word translation, smooth translation. 533pp. 6½ × 9¼. (USO) 21866-X Pa. $8.95

COUNTRY AND SUBURBAN HOMES OF THE PRAIRIE SCHOOL PERIOD, H.V. von Holst. Over 400 photographs floor plans, elevations, detailed drawings (exteriors and interiors) for over 100 structures. Text. Important primary source. 128pp. 8⅜ × 11¼. 24373-7 Pa. $5.95

CATALOG OF DOVER BOOKS

READY-TO-USE BORDERS, Ted Menten. Both traditional and unusual interchangeable borders in a tremendous array of sizes, shapes, and styles. 32 plates. 64pp. 8¼ × 11.   23782-6 Pa. $3.50

THE WHOLE CRAFT OF SPINNING, Carol Kroll. Preparing fiber, drop spindle, treadle wheel, other fibers, more. Highly creative, yet simple. 43 illustrations. 48pp. 8¼ × 11.   23968-3 Pa. $2.50

HIDDEN PICTURE PUZZLE COLORING BOOK, Anna Pomaska. 31 delightful pictures to color with dozens of objects, people and animals hidden away to find. Captions. Solutions. 48pp. 8¼ × 11.   23909-8 Pa. $2.25

QUILTING WITH STRIPS AND STRINGS, H.W. Rose. Quickest, easiest way to turn left-over fabric into handsome quilt. 46 patchwork quilts; 31 full-size templates. 48pp. 8¼ × 11.   24357-5 Pa. $3.25

NATURAL DYES AND HOME DYEING, Rita J. Adrosko. Over 135 specific recipes from historical sources for cotton, wool, other fabrics. Genuine premodern handicrafts. 12 illustrations. 160pp. 5⅜ × 8½.   22688-3 Pa. $2.95

CARVING REALISTIC BIRDS, H.D. Green. Full-sized patterns, step-by-step instructions for robins, jays, cardinals, finches, etc. 97 illustrations. 80pp. 8¼ × 11.
23484-3 Pa. $3.00

GEOMETRY, RELATIVITY AND THE FOURTH DIMENSION, Rudolf Rucker. Exposition of fourth dimension, concepts of relativity as Flatland characters continue adventures. Popular, easily followed yet accurate, profound. 141 illustrations. 133pp. 5⅜ × 8½.   23400-2 Pa. $3.00

READY-TO-USE SMALL FRAMES AND BORDERS, Carol B. Grafton. Graphic message? Frame it graphically with 373 new frames and borders in many styles: Art Nouveau, Art Deco, Op Art. 64pp. 8¼ × 11.   24375-3 Pa. $3.50

CELTIC ART: THE METHODS OF CONSTRUCTION, George Bain. Simple geometric techniques for making Celtic interlacements, spirals, Kellstype initials, animals, humans, etc. Over 500 illustrations. 160pp. 9 × 12. (Available in U.S. only)
22923-8 Pa. $6.00

THE TALE OF TOM KITTEN, Beatrix Potter. Exciting text and all 27 vivid, full-color illustrations to charming tale of naughty little Tom getting into mischief again. 58pp. 4¼ × 5½. (USO)   24502-0 Pa. $1.75

WOODEN PUZZLE TOYS, Ed Sibbett, Jr. Transfer patterns and instructions for 24 easy-to-do projects: fish, butterflies, cats, acrobats, Humpty Dumpty, 19 others. 48pp. 8¼ × 11.   23713-3 Pa. $2.50

MY FAMILY TREE WORKBOOK, Rosemary A. Chorzempa. Enjoyable, easy-to-use introduction to genealogy designed specially for children. Data pages plus text. Instructive, educational, valuable. 64pp. 8¼ × 11.   24229-3 Pa. $2.50

Prices subject to change without notice.

Available at your book dealer or write for free catalog to Dept. GI, Dover Publications, Inc., 31 East 2nd St. Mineola, N.Y. 11501. Dover publishes more than 175 books each year on science, elementary and advanced mathematics, biology, music, art, literary history, social sciences and other areas.